WARSHAA BUNA JIIDHA FI GOGA
OBBO ISIRAEEL DAGGAFA
እስራኤል ደገፋ

Coffeeography

The Coffee Producers

Stephen Philip Leighton

Published by Has Bean Coffee Publishing trading Has Bean Coffee Ltd

Has Bean Coffee Limited
Unit 16 Ladford Covert
Ladfordfields Industrial Estate
Seighford
Stafford
ST18 9QL
United Kingdom

http://www.coffeeography.co.uk

Ordering Information:
Quantity sales. Special discounts are available on quantity purchases by corporations, associations, and others. For details, contact the publisher at the address above.
Printed in the European Union.

Publisher's Cataloging-in-Publication data
Leighton, Stephen Philip
A title of a book : Coffeeography, The coffee Producers
ISBN 978-1-9997926-0-2

First Edition

My name is Stephen Leighton, and I have the best job in the world. I travel the world exploring coffee farms and searching out the world's tastiest coffee. I have more offers from people to carry my luggage on my trips than I could ever possibly need.

I have met some of the most amazing coffee farmers in the world on my travels. They all have interesting back stories and bags full of experience in the world of coffee.

I'd like to take you all on my journeys so you can meet these farmers, but alas that would be expensive and impractical. So I have written this book where you get to find out a little bit more about these super interesting people, and where I can share some of the tens of thousands of photographs I've taken with them.

We work with so many producers that we could not include them all (maybe we'll do a second volume). But with every journey there is the first step, so let's walk. Join me on this journey around the coffee world, see inside the minds of coffee producers and share with me the wonderful experiences I have had whilst meeting them.

Bolivia

“Bolivia is unique. If you go to El Salvador, it looks a little like Guatemala; if you go to Rwanda, it looks a little like Burundi; but if you go to Bolivia, it looks like space!”

– Stephen Leighton

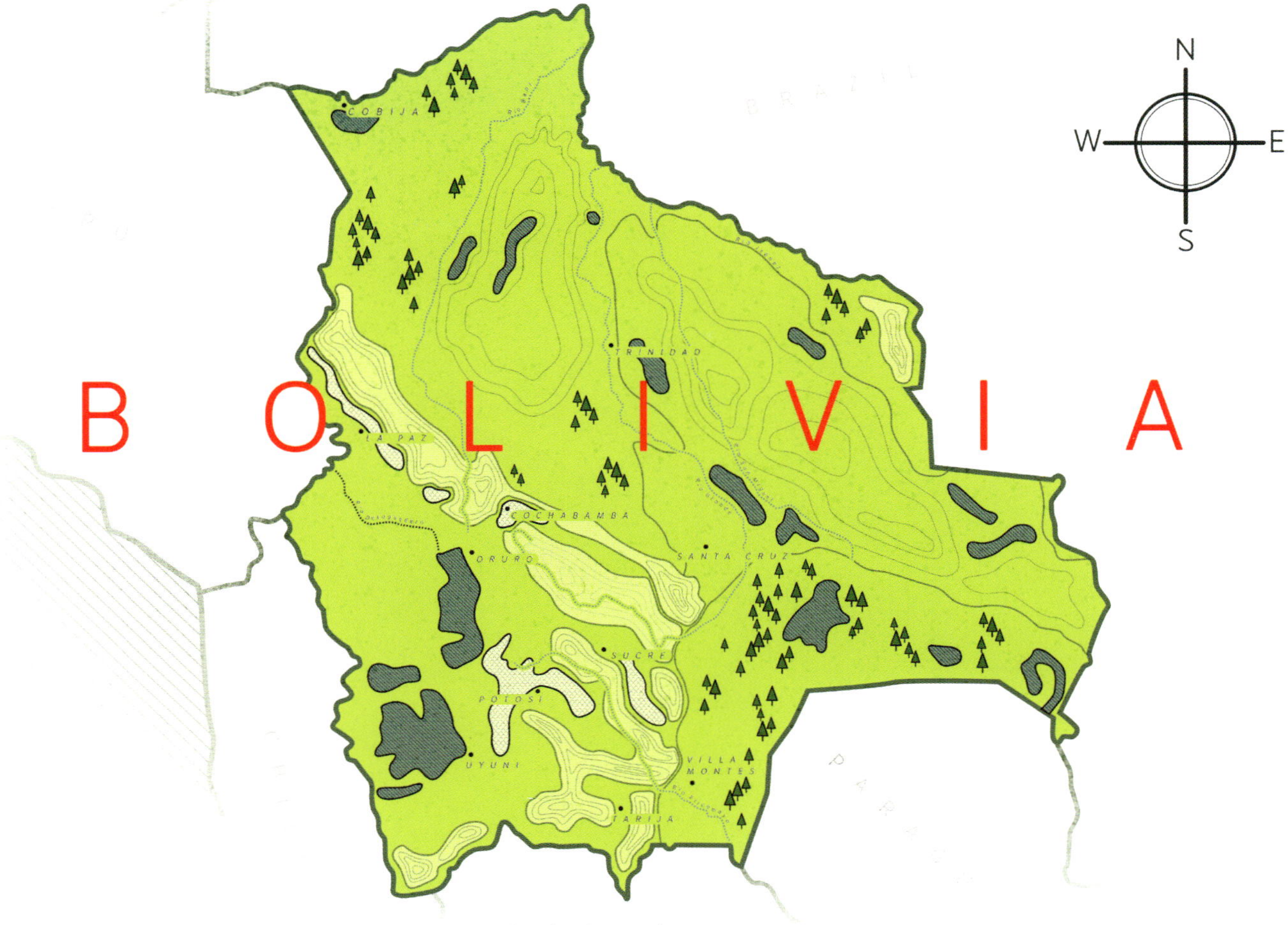

BOLIVIA

Bolivia is one of the origins for which I'm most proud of the work that Has Bean has done. When I first visited in 2006, it is fair to say Bolivia was a forgotten origin. It's a country I have visited every year since then, and it's one of the most exciting countries – and for me, it has the most potential.

Coinciding with my first visit, I got to see a change of regime firsthand in Bolivia with President Morales coming to power. The country's first president from the indigenous population, Morales' administration has focused on the removal of the influence of the United States, and he has a socialist approach in his politics, as well as a desire to support indiginous coca growers. Isolating itself from the rest of the world has made doing business in this difficult, landlocked country even harder.

Coffee production has been on the decline in Bolivia for many years, but the lack of exports, increase in coca production (legal in Bolivia) and lack of coffee infrastructure means that Bolivia's total coffee production is smaller than that of some medium-sized Brazilian farms.

Coffee production in Bolivia is mostly concentrated in the rural areas of the Yungas, where approximately 95% of the cultivation occurs.

Coffee Facts

Total production in 2016 (60 kg): 90,000
Percentage rise and fall on previous year: +0.9%
Internal consumption in 2016 (60 kg): 60,000
Consumption per capita: 0.34 kg per person per annum
Taste profile: Sweet, balanced and clean
Common varietals: Typica, Caturra and Catuai
Coffee growing altitudes: 600 m.a.s.l. to 2,200 m.a.s.l.
Rank of coffee production: 38th in the world
Main buyers: Germany, Switzerland and the United States
Unique problems: Inadequate road infrastructure, legal coca production
Soil types: west: desertic; centre: savanna; east: Amazonian forest

Country Facts

Population:
11,052,864 (2017)

Population density:
10 people per km^2

Capital city:
Sucre

Land mass:
1,078,090 km^2

Currency:
Bolivian boliviano

BOLIVIA

Machacamarca

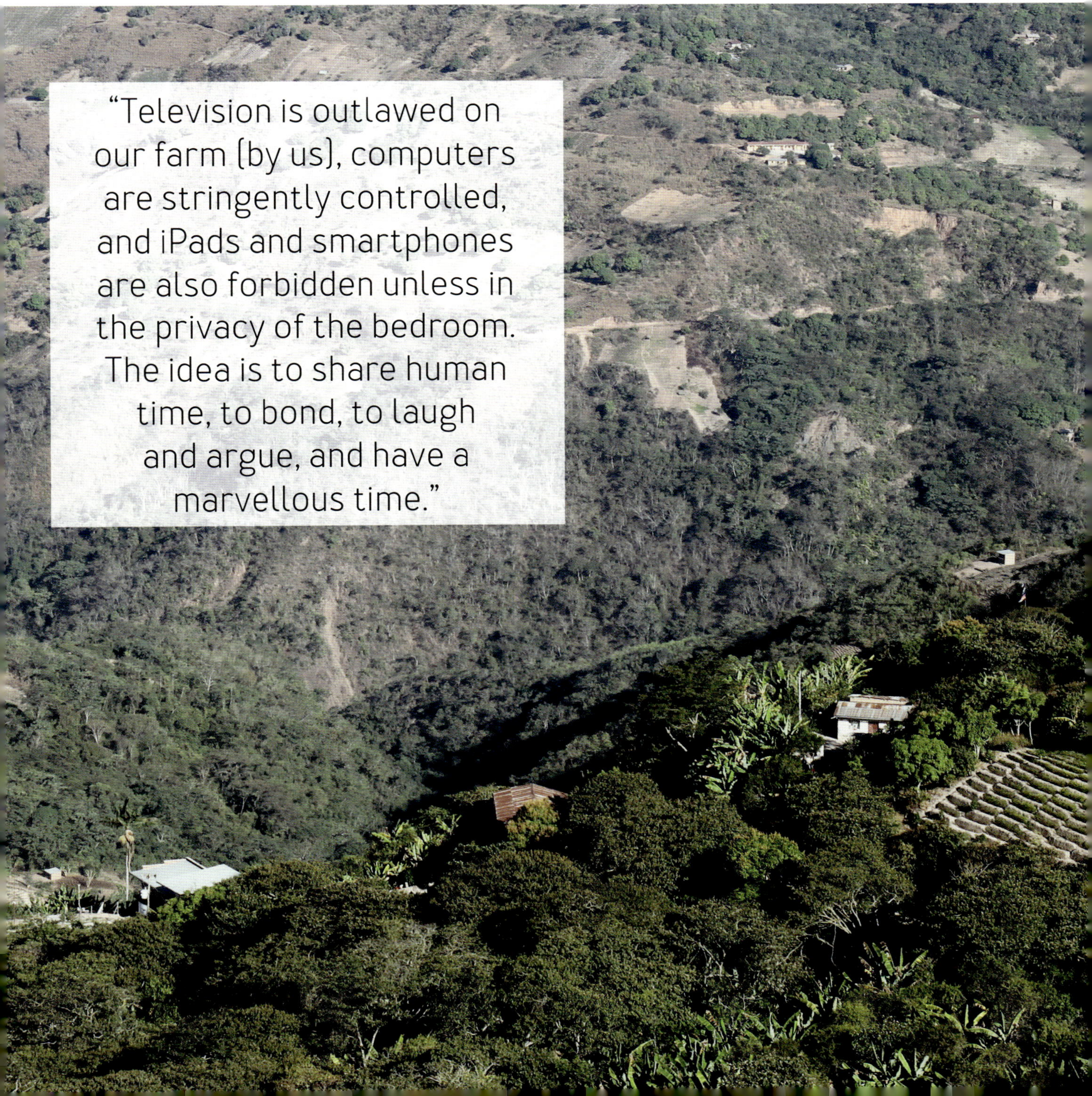

"Television is outlawed on our farm (by us), computers are stringently controlled, and iPads and smartphones are also forbidden unless in the privacy of the bedroom. The idea is to share human time, to bond, to laugh and argue, and have a marvellous time."

"Machacamarca is our traditional family property and we have been drinking our own coffee for over fifty years."

Lupe Andrede

This should be an Andrade family post, but that would take up the whole of the book. Lupe has led a very varied and eventful life: she has been a journalist (a columnist for a La Paz daily paper); she has written nine books; and she had her own television news program – and then we get to the even more interesting part of her life.

Lupe was arrested and held without due process for exposing corruption in the transitional government. She unjustly served a sentence in a Bolivian women's prison, and was under country arrest for much of the 2000s with her travel documents seized. Since her acquittal, Lupe has given talks around the world talking about this ordeal.

The Andrade family have been involved in agriculture in the Yungas region of Bolivia for many generations on the Machacamarca farm. There are documents dating back to 1865 detailing the family's activities; most interesting is an inventory that includes the house and chapel which are still standing on the farm today.

> " When we first met Stephen, we found him adventurous and charged with energy. I did not realise how deep and nearly fanatical his dedication was to coffee, when right there on our dining table he pulled out scales to weigh as I remember 22 precise grams of coffee, which would be steeped in some equally precise number of seconds."

The Yungas is a Bolivian province in an area that produced, and still produces, traditionally-grown coca leaf, which has been chewed or brewed as a herbal tea for millennia. It was so popular for its healing properties that it was distributed throughout the entire Inca Empire. However, in modern times it has been discovered that cocaine can be chemically extracted from coca leaf, which has unfortunately "tainted" the concept of coca leaf growing. Production is legal in southern Yungas, but Lupe and Mario (Lupe's brother) don't believe that it is an ideal crop any more, and do not cultivate coca. Instead, as an example to their neighbours, they have planted citrus trees, avocados and mangoes on a small commercial scale.

But the citrus trees got a blight in the early 2000s, and Lupe and Mario decided to extend the coffee production that had only been for family consumption until then.

The farm's story isn't a smooth one; it has just as much intrigue as Lupe's life. 2007 saw Machacamarca place in the Cup of Excellence with its first crop, and the coffee found an international buyer in me. Used by Colin Harmon in the 2009 World Barista Championships, Machacamarca's coffee placed 4th and seemed a roaring success.

Machacamarca's was the first coffee I bought outright from Bolivia, and it was from the farm's first ever outturn. It was also the first farm I was able to buy every bag from. That was such an exciting thing for a small roaster.

Next came something from a movie script. The farm was taken from the family by the local community. Threats of violence against them and their inability to gain access to the farm meant three years of court battles. Now it's back in family hands, and they have returned to pick up the pieces. Slowly the farm is recovering, and each year we hope that we will see coffee again from this farm. Stay tuned for the next exciting instalment from Machacamarca.

NAME: Lupe Andrade

AGE: 79

IN COFFEE: 20+ yrs

Your biggest influence in coffee: My grandmother, María. Everyone else in the family drank coffee, of course, but she was an exigent purist, and her love for the fresh and pure brew is something both Mario and I have inherited.

Your proudest achievement in coffee: Without a doubt, having met Stephen and selling our coffee to him. He has been an enormous inspiration and encouragement.

Biggest challenge facing you today: Climate change. In the past few years we have had to contend with drought, heavy rains, and something we had not seen before: hailstorms, which wrecked our crops two years running. Another problem is the crafty parrots that fly in large noisy bands and land on a coffee plant silently, and just as silently leave it devoid of cherries in a matter of minutes.

Favourite way to relax: I read a lot: everything from murder mysteries to biographies, and history to anthropology.

If you could grow coffee anywhere in the world apart from your own country, where and why: Stratford-on-Avon, or thereabouts. It would be heaven, because Shakespeare is my passion. I would come drink coffee with him in the churchyard where he's buried.

Favourite coffee varietal and why: Arábiga, because of its historic associations with Machacamarca and the Yungas region.

BOLIVIA

Finca Canton Uyunense

"My three oldest children – Silvia, Beto and Ovidio – have their own land and produce coffee. We work together. For example, in one day we clean one farm, and the next day we clean the other farm. We work as a team."

"I remember Stephen always wearing football shirts. One of my best memories is when we took the picture wearing our football shirts."

Teodocio Mamani

Teodocio and I have two things in common: our love of coffee (obviously) and our love of football. It's his love of football that brought us much closer together, but which also managed to allow him to reclaim his farm from "squatters" who took his father-in-law's farm when he passed away.

It's a story that really highlights some of the unique problems of Bolivia, and how sport can bring a community together to make sure that the right thing is finally done.

The law in rural Bolivia is something that's managed by the colonies and the local communities. The police's reach is often limited due to the sheer size of the areas and the strong community ties.

When Teodocio's father passed away, both he and his wife were left the farm that's located in Canton Uyunense – a colony that is located in the municipality of Caranavi, around 25 km from town. It's accessed by a small road that often gets blocked, making access from the outside world even harder.

Canton Uyunense has a football team, so Teodocio started playing for them.

Ever the modest, he told me he was a "good player" – such a good player that he became a fixture in the team. The locals grew to like Teodocio and decided that the "squatters" on his farm should be evicted, and that the farmers should take control of the farm that was rightly theirs. He's been there ever since.

The football links do not stop there. The first time I met Teodocio was on my visit to Bolivia in 2012. We had already bought his coffee and loved it, and he and I clicked straight away, but there was a problem in the back of my mind.

"My dream was that my children could study and live in the city. But they did not like the city and they returned back to the farm."

We had asked for some promotional photos of the farm and the family the year before, and he had a Chelsea shirt on in the pictures. Now, everyone knows Sunderland are the greatest team in the world, so I went about brainwashing Teodocio. He told me he only wore the shirt because the local team wears blue, but he would promise to follow Sunderland from now on. We even sent him a shirt to make sure.

This is a super small farm with just 6,000 plants on two hectares of land. It has a mixture of Catuai and Typica varietals, both red and yellow. Teodocio also has one hectare of land that is natural forest reserve, in which he owns a house where he lives with his wife and two youngest children. He is also planting a new area, which we should see start to produce coffee in the next couple of years.

Teodocio is unusual for a Bolivian coffee farmer, because he processes the majority of his coffee on the farm.

He does this because of the isolation of Uyunense; some days he cannot get the cherry to the mill in Caranavi. It's a real skill to be able to process such high quality on a small scale – but while he is a good footballer, he's an even better coffee producer.

NAME: Teodocio Mamani

AGE: 55

IN COFFEE: 30 yrs

Your biggest influence in coffee: My wife.
Your proudest achievement in coffee: The house that I have in La Paz city. It's thanks to coffee that I have that house where I can go with my family for holidays.
Favourite coffee varietal and why: I like Red Catuai as it seems resistant to disease and also has a very good production.
Biggest challenge facing you today: Diseases to my coffee plants, chicken eye and leaf rust.
Favourite way to relax: Any sports, but football in particular. I still play most days at 55 years old.
What makes your coffee special: The weeding that I do in my coffee plantations.
What's your favourite coffee time of the year: All Saints' Day on the 1st of November. The harvest is complete and I go to visit my father and family.
If you had a blank cheque, what would be the one investment you would make in the farm: I'd like to retire to my farm and relax, and let someone else do the hard work.

BOLIVIA

Finca Don Carlos

"We built the wet mill and began to train producers to produce specialty coffee. It was a challenge to make them understand that coffee would be paid for according to quality and we would only buy red cherries."

"I'm most proud to see the producers of Sol de Mañana are motivated and happy to continue working with coffee, and that I was part of this program."

Carlos Mariaca

Carlos is quite unique in this book. He is not a coffee farm owner like most of the others in these pages. He works with our exporter in Bolivia, Pedro Rodriguez (pictured above), as his mill manager in Caranavi. He's responsible for many of the amazing coffees coming out of this region, so I felt he had to be included in this collection of amazing producers.

But he does farm with some of the coffees we buy from Pedro, and in the past five years Carlos has also become a farm manager for a number of these farms (in fact he's had one of the farms named after him: Finca Don Carlos).

Carlos is one of the most skilled coffee people I've ever met. What Carlos doesn't know about coffee production and processing really isn't worth knowing. He's a walking library of amazing information.

Thirty years ago Carlos was a truck driver who moved roasted coffee around La Paz, but Pedro spotted his hard work and dedication to his job.

Pedro invited Carlos to come on a journey with him to build a coffee mill in the town of Caranavi. You can read about Pedro in this collection of producers, but I think it's fair to say that one of the pair can't be talked about without the other. Carlos is Pedro's right-hand man at the mill, the farms and the nursery.

"I used to be a truck driver and delivered roasted coffee in La Paz. But I moved to Caranavi and I was invited to work with Don Pedro. We built the wet mill and trained producers to produce specialty coffee. It was a challenge to make them understand that coffee would be paid for according to quality and we would only buy red cherries."

I've never met such a hard-working man. It doesn't matter what time of day I am at the mill in Caranavi, because he is always there: when I wake up, when I go to bed, or during the day. I've spoken to him about this in the past. I always visit during the harvest, and his family are fairly used to not seeing him during this time. He promises me that he does spend more time at home out of season, but I'm not sure I believe him.

You see, around five years ago Pedro took on a new project of starting his own farms. Yield had been drastically falling for many years in Bolivia as people abandoned coffee farms for growing the legal and lucrative coca leaf (the one used in the production of cocaine). This decline seriously affected the mill.

So Pedro and Carlos went about buying virgin plots of farm land and planting new coffee plants, but not on a normal, sensible scale; rather, in a huge and very exciting way.

Buying a total of seven farms, they spent much of what would normally be the resting season preparing some of the most picturesque and well-organised farms I've seen anywhere in the world. They planted the farms with exotic varietals like Bourbon, Longberry and Geisha. I feel like I've been part of the journey with them, seeing these farms grow from unmanaged land to full production coffee farms.

Using all of Carlos' expertise (learnt from working with all the producers delivering to the mill in Caranavi over many years), and all of Pedro's coffee knowledge and marketing experience, they have successfully begun to produce some of the most exciting coffee I've ever tasted from Bolivia.

It's amazing to see the work that Carlos has done, and how integral he is to the Rodriguez family.

NAME: Carlos Mariaca

AGE: 59

IN COFFEE: 30 yrs

Your biggest influence in coffee: My wife and my farms.
Favourite coffee varietal and why: Catuai. Good production, and the plant always looks healthy and nice the whole year.
Biggest challenge facing you today: Leaf rust.
Favourite way to relax: I love mornings. I like to wake up early and go to the farms, sit next to a tree (meditate), and breathe fresh air.
Tell us a funny moment working with Stephen: Playing football with Steve in Illimani colony. I was playing in an international team – with Stephen it was a combination of different nationalities and cultures on one football court.
What's your favourite coffee time of the year? Harvest time. I like to work hard. There is a dynamic working with producers and clients. I also enjoy seeing the farm in production – seeing people picking the beans. Also I enjoy the satisfaction of seeing all the work that I did for the whole year come to fruition.

BOLIVIA

Finca Vicente Paye

"My dog Copito is usually very aggressive and barks at everybody. But when Stephen arrives, Copito just goes to Stephen and hugs him without barking at all. It is like my dog recognises Stephen and is waiting for him."

"I moved to Copacabana when I was six years old. I remember that there were no roads. My father was one of the colony founders."

Vicente Paye

Vicente is a success story – a success in a country where the coffee industry has had far too few successes. I first tasted this coffee as part of a blend from producers of the small colony of Copacabana. The blend was fantastic, but then we got an opportunity to taste the contributors by individual cups, and the rest is history.

Vicente is located in Copacabana, which lies about 180 km from La Paz in the heart of the Caranavi which is recognised as one of the leading coffee-producing regions in Bolivia.

The colony of Copacabana has a collection of small farms that are normally around five hectares in size (although Vicente has ten hectares). The farm ranges over an altitude of 1,550 to 1,600 metres above sea level (m.a.s.l.), and it benefits from the amazing environment of Caranavi and its rich coffee growing history.

So why is Vicente a success story? Bolivia has all the things in place to produce amazing coffee: fertile soils, climate and altitude. Despite its international recognition amongst coffee people,

“My children were born in La Paz. It was very difficult for them to move to Caranavi at first. They did not like it at all. But when the project Sol de Mañana started, my family became more involved. Now they help me on the farm, and they are eager to see the new plantations – and Stephen, when he is visiting us.”

Caranavi has neglected its coffee production. A mixture of ageing coffee plantations, reducing yields and leaf rust, combined with a high pressure towards coca cultivation, has meant coffee has been in decline. With coca being four times more profitable and encountering less growing issues, it has meant many producers have abandoned coffee production in favour of the more lucrative crop.

To try to save specialty coffee in Caranavi, our exporter Pedro Rodriguez started the project “Sol de Mañana.” He has been sourcing coffee from small producers in the region for three decades. However, this steady decline of coffee production has not only put the sustainability of his export business at risk, but the future of coffee production in Bolivia is at risk of disappearing forever.

Vicente is the first to emerge as a superstar from Sol de Mañana, taking on agronomic advice, replanting old plant stock, working the land and tackling farming head on – not “just letting it happen.”

This has meant an uplift in production, happiness, and most importantly (to me) quality and (to him) profit.

There was a knock-on effect neither of us saw coming. His daughter (pictured with the parrot) was not a big fan of the coffee farm. She saw it as a drain on her father’s time, and an obstacle to them spending time as a family. That was until she found an article and video of her father talking about the farm on some English coffee website.

This made her so proud that when she had to present who was her hero at school, she quite rightly chose her father. I love visiting the whole family, but in particular his children; they are so excited and inquisitive about what we are doing to market their coffee. And, through hard work, they do have an amazing coffee to market.

He is a true coffee Hero in every sense of the word.

NAME: Vicente Paye

AGE: 51

IN COFFEE: 30 yrs

What's your favourite coffee time of the year: July to September – HARVEST TIME! As a producer, this is the time when I receive payment for all my hard work.

Your proudest achievement in coffee: I have an advanced production model compared to my neighbours, and I see my plants growing and producing much more than theirs. This makes me very proud.

Biggest challenge facing you today: Today I am facing health problems and because of that I could not plant from my (plant) nursery this year. I was at the hospital for four months, which has set the farm back.

Favourite way to relax: I love mornings. I like to wake up and walk through the forest smelling pure air.

Favourite coffee varietal and why: Catuai. It's a variety that does not rest. The production is very consistent year by year.

What makes your coffee special: I control my coffee from diseases and plagues. I have good management of my plantation. All the picking is well selected and without green cherries.

BOLIVIA

Finca Las Alasitas

"For me it is amazing. Steve is always excited (the altitude and the arrival time don't matter). So much so that he has to bike the Death Road every time he comes to Bolivia."

"We were lucky! We are a passionate coffee family and we love what we do. Coffee keeps us together."

Daniela Rodriguez

By her own admission, Daniela was born into coffee, and her earliest memories are of her father's involvement in coffee. Her father is recognised as one of the most influential men in coffee (and you can read about him in this book), but I think Pedro would be the first to agree that none of it would have been possible without his children.

Daniela recalls: "All our holidays, we used to travel to Los Yungas to be with my father during the harvest."

When she was seventeen years old, Pedro took Daniela to the SCAA (Specialty Coffee Association of America) to help him try to introduce Bolivian coffee to an international audience. At that moment she knew she would work with him in coffee.

After university, she did indeed work with Pedro, running the office. But the opportunity to work in Spain arose; it was a chance to travel (one of Daniela's passions) and experience a new country and culture.

"Steve is always wearing something red, and is always with a new gadget."

But the lure of coffee and Bolivia was too strong, and two years later she was back working in the business.

I've tried a number of times to find out Daniela's job title, but I think it's "everything": from. client liaison to logistics, to making sure the cuppings are set up, and making sure the menu's up-to-date for tomorrow's breakfast.

And she has the hardest commute in the world. Although Caranavi is only 180 km from La Paz, it may as well be on a different planet given there is the worst road in the world between them. The road is open from 5 p.m. at night until 6 a.m. in the morning, and traversing it can take anything from 2–3 hours to over 12 hours, depending on how many times the road gets blocked.

Undeterred, Daniela makes the journey every few days in June through to September, ferrying potential customers backwards and forwards to the family's state-of-the-art mill in the heart of Caranavi town.

She also acts as the very important translator between her father and the stupid green buyers who speak no Spanish (read that as being me). She also has a tight grip on their cupping lab and samples from the mill, pulling every string of the operation together.

Daniela's instrumental in the development of the program of new farms to supplement the ever dwindling production in the region. The farms have new plant tissue, new varietals and a new farming approach, and they're set up to not only produce amazing coffee, but to show local people that there is a future in coffee farming for Bolivia.

Daniela is a link between the coffee world and the amazing coffees of Bolivia. Without her family, Bolivian coffee could have virtually disappeared; without Daniela, the rest of the coffee world wouldn't have known about the revolution going on in the Bolivian specialty coffee world thanks to this superhero family.

NAME: Daniela Rodriguez

AGE: 31

IN COFFEE: 31 yrs

Your biggest influence in coffee: My father, of course. His passion and drive to improve Bolivian coffee is infectious.

Your proudest achievement in coffee: Seeing our coffee in the finest coffee shops around the world.

Biggest challenge facing you today: The decrease in coffee production that Bolivia is facing.

Favourite coffee varietal and why: I love the Java varietal: delicate, floral, a nice cup profile and a good yield of production. But the best attribute is the form of the tree. It is very nice, like a Christmas tree.

If you could grow coffee anywhere in the world apart from your own country, where and why: I believe it would be Panama, because is has all the conditions to produce good coffee. It is a safe country and is near the ocean.

What's your favourite coffee time of the year: It has to be harvest time. It's our busiest time of the year, but all our friends visit us from around the world and the coffee plants look so nice with the red or yellow cherries.

BOLIVIA

Finca La Linda

"I have the luck to work with my two kids. Since they finished university, they feel a passion for coffee and making things better."

"It has been a wonderful experience to be part of the transformation that Bolivia has had in the context of the specialty coffee market."

Pedro Rodriguez

Pedro is a rare man: a businessman, intelligent, thoughtful, caring, and in Bolivia. In my eleven years of visiting Bolivia, the country has changed beyond recognition. The political situation has taken a lean towards the left, and ties with the USA and other big markets have been broken, which has left the economy in a difficult position.

While all this has happened, Pedro has ploughed a lonely furrow in the world of specialty coffee in Bolivia.

Pedro's story starts in commercial coffee, not specialty. Thirty years ago he worked as an exporter. After ten years doing this, he saw that yields were dropping and the coffee business was getting harder.

Not taking the easy option but instead using it as inspiration, he decided to go into farming himself.

When Pedro began farming, he decided to focus on the commercial side of the coffee industry and pursued certifications like "Organic," because he believed it was the only way to get extra money for the coffee he was selling.

“In the mountains of the Andes, the production of the small producers from whom I bought was declining steadily. This was when I made the decision to produce specialty coffee in the mountains. Now I have small farms above 1,500 m.a.s.l. with more than 30 different varieties.”

This was at the beginning of the specialty revolution in the world, and it had most certainly not hit Bolivia at that time.

Bolivia has all the ingredients to have some of the best coffees in the world: altitude, volcanic soils, and a country full of hard-working farmers who tame the harsh and mountainous land. Pedro spotted this gap in the market and decided to act as the bridge between specialty buyers and the smallholder farmers.

Pedro decided to build a mill in Caranavi where small coffee producers could deliver their cherries, and where he could process the cherries and find the route to market.

This proved very successful, and he built up this market with the help of his mill manager and friend, Carlos Mariaca. This led to an amazing explosion of super special coffees from the region.

In 2006 there was a change of government, which meant that exporting became more of a challenge for this landlocked country. Not only this, but there was a push for coffee farmers to turn their land over to the much more productive and lucrative growing of coca. Although the growing of coca is completely legal and traditional in Bolivia, growing the plant is harsh on the soil, and it is only a short-term crop until it renders the soil useless for growing anything.

Bolivia has seen a drastic drop in coffee production in recent years, and there is a devastating drop in coffee being delivered to Pedro’s mill in Caranavi.

Pedro sees every problem as a challenge. He decided to address the problem head on by investing in seven coffee farms in a short space of time, to fill the capacity of the mill and show local people that there is a future for coffee growing in the region.

The farms produced their first commercial crop this year, and the example of planting exotic varietals and farming with care and understanding of the environment means the future of Bolivian coffee remains in Pedro’s hands.

NAME: Pedro Rodiguez

AGE: 51

IN COFFEE: 31 yrs

Your biggest influence in coffee: The nature and the environment that offers Los Yungas.

Your proudest achievement in coffee: To have the opportunity to influence the fact that Bolivia is seen as providing some of the best coffee in the world.

Biggest challenge facing you today: To try to increase the production of coffee in Bolivia.

Tell us a funny moment working with Stephen, or how you met and the first meeting: I am impressed by the crazy things he does, like arriving in La Paz at more than 3,600 m.a.s.l. at 3 a.m., and descending to 1,000 m.a.s.l. by bicycle on the famous Road of Death at 6 a.m.

If you could grow coffee anywhere in the world apart from your own country, where and why? Panama or Costa Rica, because they have all the conditions to produce good coffee and security.

If you had a blank cheque, what would be the one investment you would make in the farm? I would invest in a spring to have consistent water for the farm.

Brazil

"Brazil is often dismissed in the speciality world because of its size and its huge production. But when you produce so much coffee, how can there not be amazing quality?"

– Stephen Leighton

B R A Z I L

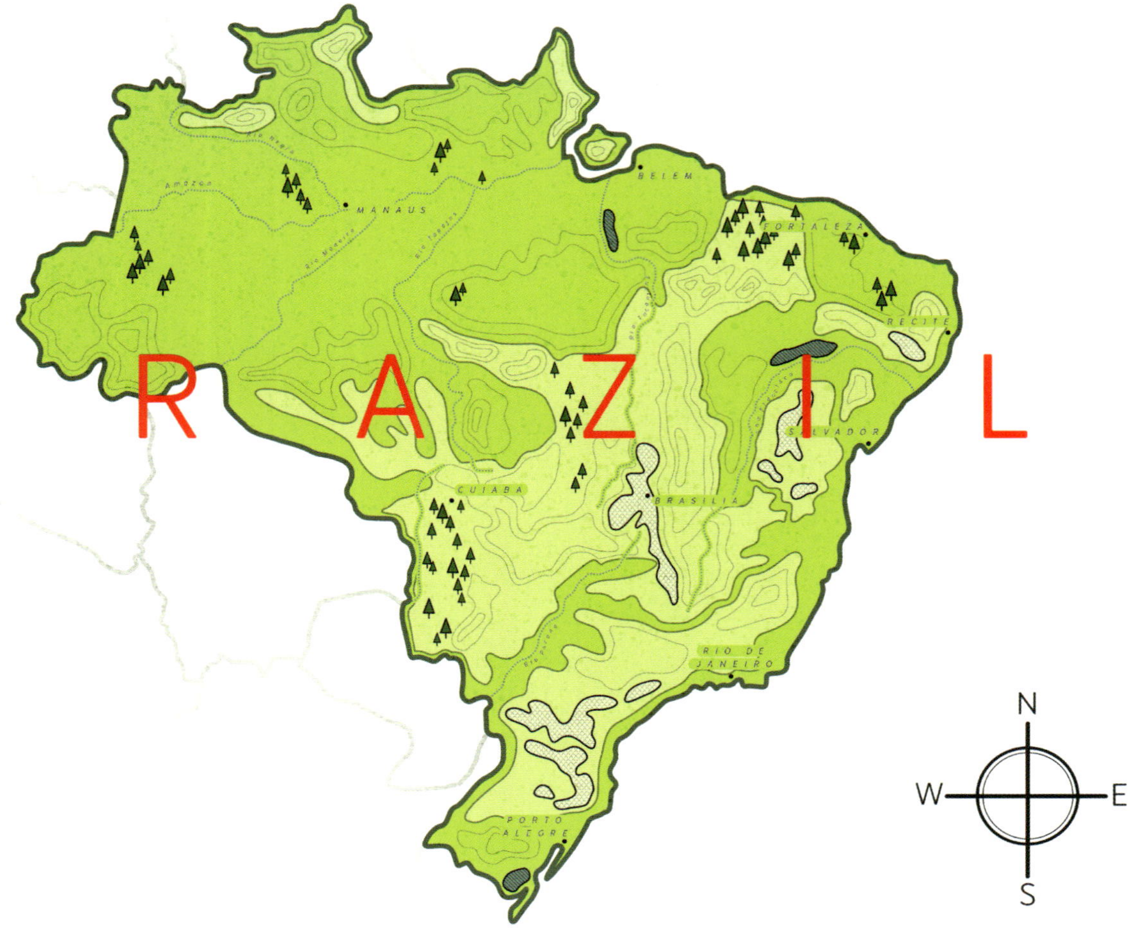

Brazil is a superpower in the world of coffee. Brazil produces nearly 33% of all the coffee grown, with over 27,000 km² of land devoted to coffee production.

Coffee was first established here in the 1720s, and it is surrounded by myth and legend. It is claimed that Francisco de Melo Palheta, a Lieutenant Colonel in the Portuguese army, smuggled the seeds from French Guiana after a diplomatic visit to the country regarding land borders. Portugal was keen to get involved in the lucrative coffee production that was growing around the colonised world, and so sent de Melo Palheta on a secret mission.

The most romantic version of this story is that Francisco used his handsome good looks to befriend Marie-Claude de Vicq de Pontgibaud, the wife of a French governor. It is said that on his final night in French Guiana, he was given a bouquet of flowers that contained cuttings from a coffee plant.

However it was introduced, as the Frank Sinatra song says, "They've got an awful lot of coffee in Brazil." And with volume there has to be not just some quality. For me, Brazil has some of the most underrated specialty coffee in the world, and some amazing producers and familiar profiles that are loved by coffee drinkers.

Coffee Facts

Total production in 2016 (60 kg): 55,000,000

Percentage rise and fall on previous year: +9.2%

Internal consumption in 2016 (60 kg): 20,500,00

Consumption per capita: 5.9 kg

Taste profile: Low acidity, big body and high sweetness

Common varietals: Bourbon, Typica and Mundo Novo

Coffee growing altitudes: 500 m.a.s.l. to 1,350 m.a.s.l.

Rank of coffee production: 1st in the world

Main buyers: Worldwide

Unique problems: High staffing costs, low altitudes and a competative market.

Soil types: Terra Roxa

Country Facts

Population:
211,243,220 (2017)

Population density:
25 people per km²

Capital city:
Brasilia

Land mass:
8,349,320 km²

Currency:
Real

BRAZIL

Fazenda Cachoeira da Grama

“My father always told me you can be anything, but do it well. You can be a clown, but if you do, you have to be a good one!”

"Costs are always rising in Brazil, and it's a challenge to get a price that pays well enough to farm on the side of a mountain."

Gabriel de Carvalho Dias

Gabriel was my first love! Not in that way, but my first farmer crush way back in 2003 when I first tasted his coffee. I can remember the setting when I cupped his coffee, the time of day, and how it made me feel. It's still one of my all-time favourite coffees and from one of my all-time favourite producers.

Fazenda Cachoeira da Grama has been in the Carvalho Dias family since 1890 and recently celebrated its 122nd crop. It is located in São Paulo state, just three miles from the border with Minas Gerais state, where some of the finest Brazilian coffees are grown (in my opinion). It enjoys the typical characteristics of the mountainous Mogiana and Sul de Minas regions, and it's located at an altitude of 1,100–1,250 metres above sea level.

Gabriel de Carvalho Dias is one of Brazil's leading agronomists. His family owns several farms, and they border each other in this area. With a total area of 417 hectares, Fazenda Cachoeira da Grama has a coffee plantation area of 165 hectares.

“My favourite time of the year on the farm is during the harvest – grabbing a handful of coffee from the hot patio, and smelling that sweet caramel.”

Everything is done manually on this farm since its topography does not allow any kind of mechanisation. The mill is located close to the spa town of Poços de Caldas, which is 45 minutes away from the farm.

Gabriel's father was the only brother of eleven siblings not to work on the farm. He went to Rio de Janeiro at the age of ten to study, and he became an engineer and a mathematics doctor. His brothers only called him “the professor.” Gabriel was born in Rio, but his father would always take him to the farm for long weekends (a seven hour drive). Inspired by these farm visits and a love of nature, Gabriel decided to study agronomy. He has one sister who is a veterinarian, and one who is a biologist.

Once qualified, Gabriel moved to Goiás state, located in the heart of Brazil, and began a soybean farm using his agronomy skills. He remained there until 1993.

His grandmother, who had been a widow since 1955, lived on her own managing the family farm until a great age. She attended Gabriel's wedding one month before she turned 100. She died at 103 years old in 1991, so her eleven siblings decided to divide the farm. They did so peacefully, completing the plan in December 1993, when Gabriel ended up owning Cachoeira.

Beginning in January 1994, he moved to the farm and entered the coffee business. Surrounded by family who had years of coffee growing experience, Gabriel took his foundations of soybean growing and agronomy to create one of the most famous and successful coffee farms in Brazil.

Achieving 1st place in the Illy Espresso Competition in 1999 was a proud moment for Gabriel. He then went on to place every year for five years in a row in Cup of Excellence, finishing 2nd, 3rd and 4th with Fazenda Cachoeira da Grama and Rainha, which he managed.

He is one of the first “Rock Star” growers in the speciality coffee world, and he continues to produce one of the best coffees on the planet.

NAME: Gabriel de Carvalho Dias

AGE: 53

IN COFFEE: 23 yrs

Your biggest influence in coffee: It has to be my father. He always told me, "you can be anything, but do it well. You can be a clown, but if you do, you have to be a good one!"

Favourite coffee you've had (not including yours): That's a tough one. We made a coffee cupping once of fifteen different coffees from many different countries, with a group of wine-loving friends. Mine was first place unanimously, and a Jamaican Blue Mountain was second place. That's a good memory.

Biggest challenge facing you today: Sales! Costs are always rising in Brazil, and it's a challenge to get a price that pays well enough to farm on the side of a mountain.

Favourite way to relax: Sharing a good cup of coffee with friends – if it is while looking at the mountains in Fazenda Cachoeira da Grama, that makes it even better.

Favourite coffee varietal and why: Yellow Bourbon. But that's not a rule. There are other varietals that are well prepared on the patio, and which are also great.

BRAZIL

Fazenda Passeio

"If I had a blank cheque, I would transform my farm into an institute open to all people that love coffee to visit and learn."

"When I visited the Has Bean roastery in Stafford, we recorded a video for the website. It was fun but very strange at times."

Adolfo Henrique Vieira Ferreira

Adolfo is a forth generation coffee producer with over 30 years of experience in the coffee industry. His farm, Fazenda Passeio, is huge: it has 450 hectares, with 240 hectares dedicated to coffee. Fazenda Passeio produces over 4,000 bags of coffee a year; it is located at an altitude between 1,100 and 1,250 m.a.s.l., and is near to the town of Alfenas.

Fazenda Passeio can be found in the famous coffee growing region of Minas Gerais. It's a region that some of my favourite coffees in the world are from, let alone some of my favourite Brazilian coffees.

Because the farm is located on the steep mountainous slopes of Alfenas, it is impossible to farm the land with the modern machinery that many of its neighbours use. This means every bean has to be picked by hand, which is unusual for Brazil.

This challenge has made Adolfo focus on production, making sure that the coffee he produces is high quality. He uses the negative of having to pick by hand and turns it into a positive.

“I will not let something as small as a mountain stand in the way of a better coffee, a better world.”

It’s difficult to compete on price if your product is the same, and given increased labour costs it’s important to have a differentiator.

Adolfo says: “I won’t let something as small as a mountain stand in the way of a better coffee, a better world.”

Adolfo is a huge fan of experimenting and has done lots of work with different varietals, such as Mundo Novo, Catuaí, Acaiá, Icatu and Bourbon. This is driven by his desire not just to find high yielding coffee, but to find out which coffees grow best in the the unique microclimate he has on his farm.

Not only is he an experimenter, but Adolfo is also an innovator. He has been a pioneer in the development of new varietals, primarily Topázio and Rubi.

Adolfo’s farm is big, and this means he has a lot of coffee to sell. For the last sixteen years he has been a leading producer for the Illy group.

Every farm produces many different qualities, and Adolfo has encompassed specialty, commercial and commodity perfectly in one farm.

Adolfo has been awarded for his hard work by the Illy Institute of Trieste; they gave him the Illy Quality Award for the Sul de Minas region in 2014.

Adolfo also promotes the work of other Brazilian farms. He has been an active member for many years in the BSCA (the Brazilian Specialty Coffee Association).

These efforts were rewarded in 2015 with Adolfo being elected the President and Chairman of the Board of Directors of the BSCA.

Alongside all these awards and boards, Adolfo is an amazing coffee producer. Fazenda Passeio is probably one of the largest yielding farms we buy from, and it shows that quality is available from big coffee farms.

NAME: Adolfo Henrique Vieira Ferreira

AGE: 54

IN COFFEE: 33 yrs

Your biggest influence in coffee: This is between my father, Benedito Ferreira, and my cousin, Marcelo Vieira, who have both helped me develop as a coffee producer.

Your proudest achievement in coffee: Producing high quality in coffee, and introducing Fazenda Passeio coffee for partners around the world who recognise our effort.

Favourite coffee varietal and why: Topásio variety. I like its great sweetness, and it's balanced with great acidity.

Espresso or filter: Filter: it has good balance. I can drink filter coffee the whole day.

Favourite coffee you've had (not including yours): An Ethiopian Natural that was just so different.

What makes your coffee special: It is produced at 1,200 metres of altitude, with a very special microclimate. We have invested in varieties and training workers: our two most valuable resources.

Tell us a little about your family and how they are involved: My family has been involved in coffee production for more than 100 years, since my great-grandfather came from Portugal and started to work in Brazil. I am fourth generation and my sons, although young, have an interest in working in coffee production.

BRAZIL

Carmo Estate

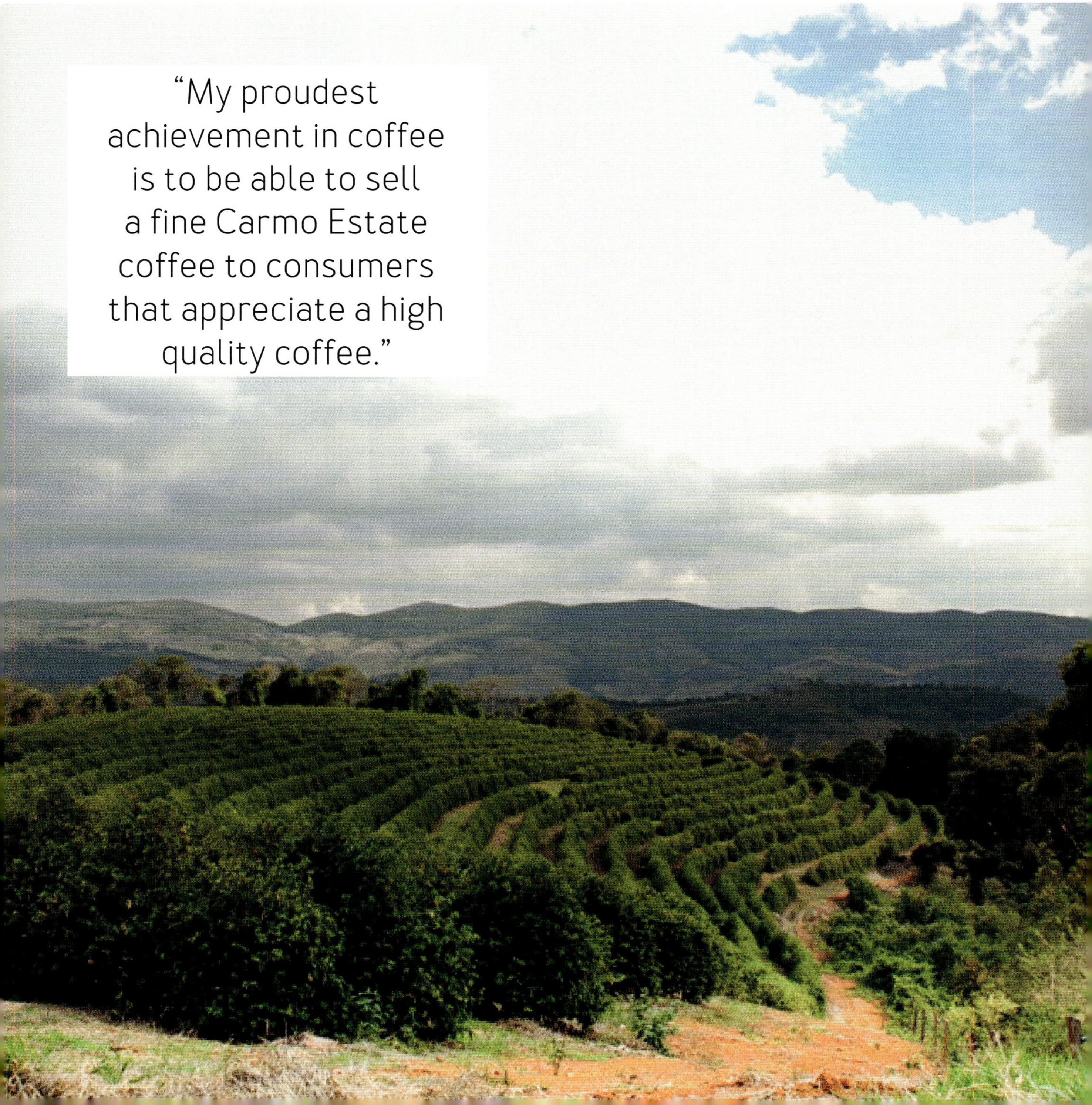

"My proudest achievement in coffee is to be able to sell a fine Carmo Estate coffee to consumers that appreciate a high quality coffee."

"My biggest influence in coffee was to transform Carmo Estate into a role model for the region in coffee quality, environmental protection and social awareness."

Tulio Henrique Renno Junqueira

The Junqueira family started growing coffee on the highlands of southern Minas Gerais 150 years ago on their farm, Fazenda Carmo. Tulio Junquiera, who represents the fifth generation of coffee growers in his family, has combined tradition with innovation to make Carmo Estate a sustainable farm.

Tulio is also a former president of the Brazil Specialty Coffee Association (BSCA): he held the role in 2009–2010.

Carmo Estate's mission is to produce exceptional coffees while providing its employees with a good quality of life and ensuring environmental sustainability.

The farm is located near the town of Heliodora in the southern state of Minas Gerais. It's a stunning region with mountainous terrain and ideal conditions to grow specialty coffees.

Carmo Estate has 220 hectares (545 acres) of land planted out with Mundo Novo, Catuaí, Catucaí, Bourbon, Acaiá and Icatú varietals.

“The most unique part is that the farm also runs an innovative profit-sharing programme, in which employees are invited to become partners in Carmo Estate.”

A combination of careful management and excellent growing conditions produce an average yield of 40 bags per hectare, which is more than twice the national average. Coffees from Carmo Estate are grown at altitudes ranging from 950 to 1,200 ma.s.l.

Tulio is unique in Brazil, from my experience. He offers on-site healthcare, schooling for children, programmes to encourage workers to build their own housing, and adult education projects and training on the importance of environmental preservation.

The most unique part is that the farm also runs an innovative profit-sharing programme, in which employees are invited to become partners in Carmo Estate, and thus become entitled to a share of the profits earned from the sale of its coffees.

The farm is producing around 7,000 bags of coffee per year. This is huge. To give you context, it's around half of the entire coffee exportation of the whole country of Bolivia.

With nearly 50% of this being specialty (3,500 bags) coffee, Tulio has to work hard to be able to find buyers and keep them.

But he also protects his brand, with the commodity coffee not being sold under the Carmo brand.

Tulio loves the relationship around selling coffee. He has many buyers because he has such a big farm, but each buyer is unique and needs a different approach.

One thing that seems to work well for him is that he loves to travel, and he has been all around the world meeting and gaining context for all the buyers with whom he works.

One of my favourite memories whilst buying coffee was watching the Brazil vs. Chile game in Tulio's living room with an ice cold beer in hand – watching on the farm, with the drying patios just outside the window. You can bet I was cheering for Brazil; I had no other choice. It's a very special memory.

NAME: Tulio Henrique Renno Junqueira

AGE: 61

IN COFFEE: 41 yrs

Favourite coffee you've had (not including yours): My "favourite one" keeps changing all the time. Tasting a new one is exciting, so I don't have a favourite!

Biggest challenge facing you today: Discovering new varietals, procedures and ways to improve year-by-year the quality of Carmo Estate coffees.

If you could grow coffee anywhere in the world apart from your own country, where and why: In 1995 I visited Costa Rica and I loved the country, the landscape, their care of the environment, and the way they grow coffee there. Someday?

Tell us a funny moment working with Stephen, or how you met and the first meeting: When Stephen visited Carmo Estate, he used a drone. When it landed on the patio, my dog, Fumaça, bit it.

If you had a blank cheque, what would be the one investment you would make in the farm: I would improve the neighbourhood of the farm. The kids could get a better education in a full-time school, more healthcare and continuous education concerning the environment.

BRAZIL

Fazenda Inglaterra

"This year our top lot Brazil Cup of Excellence entry scored 84.11 – not far shy from qualifying for Cup of Excellence. That would be the ultimate accolade – if I could get a lot into the Cup of Excellence."

"We will have made it as an industry when we can ask these ten random people to name two Arabica coffee varietals. Now we're not even close."

Stephen Hurst

I first met Stephen Hurst in 2003, and I instantly liked him. I will go as far to say that without Stephen, Has Bean wouldn't exist right now. You see, as well as being a coffee farmer, Stephen is a coffee importer, and he was the first person who took me seriously as a coffee person and gave me the courage and confidence to do what I do today.

But I also hate Stephen, because he has stolen my dream: the dream of owning your own coffee farm. Back in 2003, I was young and green in the coffee world, and Stephen had a whole heap of experience in the commodity market, but he was a few years into setting up his own coffee importing business after a successful career in Goldman Sachs as a coffee trader.

I was tasting all the coffee I could. I came across a Brazilian coffee a competitor had, and I fell in love with the coffee. I tracked down that Mercanta (Stephen's business) was the importer. So I fired an email off asking if I could buy some of this coffee. Up until this point, no one had taken me seriously; in fact, I couldn't even get samples. Stephen replied, inviting me to their lab to come cup with them one evening.

"Gabriel from Fazenda Cachoeira told me one time that in the older days, every farm would have a fool who worked there. Now I am a farmer, he says that every fool has a farm."

The rest, as they say, is history. Over the next few years, Mercanta became (and still is) a very important part of our business.

I'll let Stephen tell you the story of how he came to own "Inglaterra."

"Maybe it had always been an idea in the back of my mind. So in 2007 when some friends in Brazil mentioned that a small coffee farm was for sale, I had a look.

The farm name (Fazenda Toca Da Onca) meant "hiding place of a small wildcat." The locals now call the farm "Inglaterra." The previous owners had abandoned Toca Da Onca / Inglaterra; we had to start again, almost from scratch. Some surviving coffee trees were pruned right back and the coffee that you are now drinking is that re-growth from the original, old trees.

For the coffee people: the varietals are Icatu, Acaiá and Catucai. In future I expect coffee cherry varietals to become as well known as wine grape varietals, and to a much wider audience. The farm is located near the lovely spa town of Poços De Caldas in the coffee growing heartlands of Brazil's Minas Gerais state. The farm's elevation is 950–1,300 metres, and it has rich soil. It's on the edge of an ancient caldera / super volcano, the outline of which can be seen on satellite images. Fifty percent of the farm is virgin Mata Atlântica forest, and it will stay that way as long as I own it. I am replanting some areas with the help of my local friends Gabriel and Cristiano, without whose assistance this project would never have started."

The farm goes from strength to strength and I have bought all of this coffee since its first production, and here at Has Bean we have a worldwide exclusive on the entire harvest.

Stephen's one of my closest friends in coffee, and a true legend in the world of UK (and Brazilian) coffee. The farm is everything I'd want my project to be.

NAME: Stephen L. Hurst

AGE: 53

IN COFFEE: 32 yrs

Your biggest influence in coffee: In my early career in coffee, it was probably my old boss, Kevin Ryan, from Goldman Sachs Group. Since founding Mercanta in 1996, I have met so many top coffee producers, but one of the special ones, a real pioneer, is Gabriel de Carvalho Dias (from Fazenda Cachoeira da Grama).

Your proudest achievement in coffee: Mercanta being 20 years old in 2016 gave me a huge sense of achievement. The Financial Times feature article in March 2016 was the "icing on the cake," so to speak.

Biggest challenge facing you today: The USD to GBP£ exchange rate – not only for my importing business, but for funding the investments in the farm.

Favourite way to relax: On the farm I have a giant picnic rock with the most amazing views. It's a great place to share a single malt whisky.

If you could grow coffee anywhere in the world apart from your own country, where and why: Antioquia, Colombia. Lovely place, really great people. It has all the right topographical conditions and breathtaking scenery.

Colombia

"Colombia is a giant amongst other coffee producing countries, but unlike Brazil – where much work is done by the few – in Colombia the work is spread amongst the many."

– Stephen Leighton

C O L O M B I A

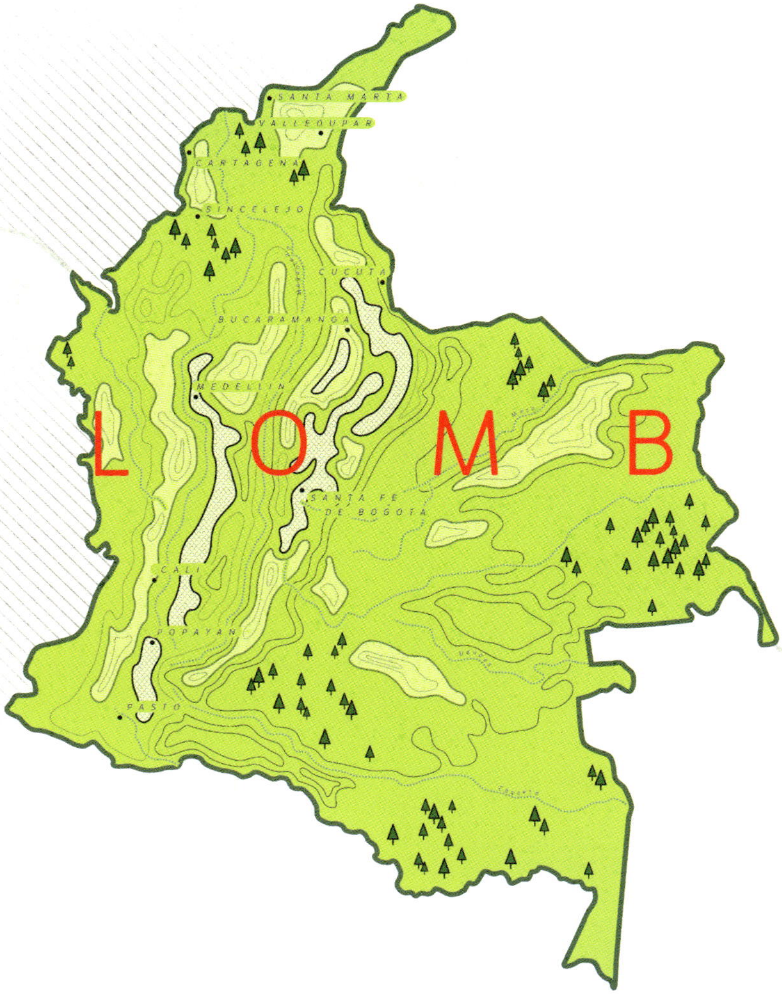

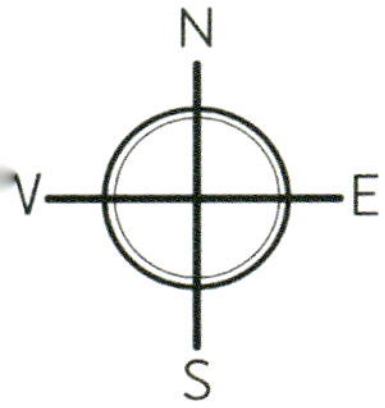

It's believed that Jesuit priests introduced coffee to Colombia around 1730, but on a very small scale. The first commercial planting can be traced to around 1835.

It was not until the second half of the 19th century that coffee production began to take off. This was because of the great expansion that the world economy underwent. Colombian landowners were able to take advantage of the emerging markets, and not only in coffee: tobacco and quinine also saw an explosion in production. Coffee made up approximately 50% of all Colombian exports by 1912.

In 1927 The National Federation of Coffee Growers of Colombia (FNC) was formed. It's a non-profit business association, and it became one of the most dominant powers in world coffee. Funded by a percentage of coffee exports, it's become a powerhouse representing more than 500,000 coffee producers, most of whom run small family-owned farms.

The FNC introduced a very successful denominations-of-origin program. It owns the world-famous Juan Valdez brand, which has been used to promote Colombian coffee all around the world since 1958.

Coffee Facts

Total production in 2016 (60 kg): 14,500,500
Percentage rise and fall on previous year: +3.5%
Internal consumption in 2016 (60 kg): 1,500,000
Consumption per capita: 1.85 kg per person per annum
Taste profile: A huge variety from dark chocolate to high fruit acidic coffees
Common varietals: Caturra. Typica, Bourbon and Cafe Colombia
Coffee growing altitudes: 1,200 m.a.s.l. to 2,100 m.a.s.l.
Rank of coffee production: 3rd in the world
Main buyers: Germany, USA and Japan
Unique problems: Drug issues, gang violence and emerging economy with big disparity
Soil types: Volcanic

Country Facts

Population:
49,067,981 (2017)

Population density:
44 people per km^2

Capital city:
Bogota

Land mass:
1,108,301 km^2

Currency:
Peso

COLOMBIA

Finca La Chorrera

"Every day I focus on improving the quality of my coffee. I work from the tree to the post-harvest process with good practices to make my coffee better."

"When I got to finally meet the person who buys my coffee, I was very satisfied and excited. That time, Stephen asked me if I could adopt him, and it was very funny. I will never forget that."

Pedro Claros

Colombia was a mystery to me in the past. I had bought coffee on a year-by-year basis, being unable to build a long-term relationship. This was due to working with importers and varying quality; one year would be good, and one year would be bad. Then I met Pedro, and it was the start of a beautiful long-term relationship.

Pedro inherited his passion for coffee production from his father who was also a coffee grower. Pedro grew up around the harvest cycle, and learned the valuable skills needed to be a good producer.

When he was young, Pedro saw his father working hard on the farm and his passion began. A love for coffee and a pride of carrying on the family tradition has made Pedro a superstar of the coffee world.

When Pedro began to grow coffee, he joined a local association and started to sell coffee to an exporter called Caravela. He entered an internal coffee cupping competition, and Pedro's coffee was highlighted as having exceptional quality and potential.

> “Something that makes me feel satisfied is that my family are very united. We all work together and we are always communicating. I feel very proud that when I’m not in the farm, my children work as if I was here and the coffee turns out to be the same as if I produced it.”

The first time I tasted Pedro’s coffee was as part of a cooperative lot in 2012 – it was a great lot called Oporapa. The following year I was lucky enough to get a tiny lot, which never made it onto the website and was sold as an exclusive to one of our lucky wholesale customers.

Since then we’ve been able to work together to focus on buying much more coffee from the farm. We taste every single day’s cuppings from the farm and either approve or reject them. We approve anything scoring between 86 and 88, and it goes into our decaf lot that we decaf at the Colombian decaffeination plant. Anything below 86 is rejected, put into a bulk lot (a Pitalito blend) and sold on to other buyers. Anything scoring 88–90 goes into our estate blend of days’ pickings, and anything over 90 goes into a special micro lot for which we pay a much higher premium and market in a special way.

This farm is located on top of a mountain at 1,735 metres above sea level. The farm contains 70% Caturra (25,000 plants), 20% Colombia F6 (7,000 plants) and 10% Castillo (2,000 plants). The farm consists of eight hectares, six of which are planted with coffee. The other two hectares house the mill and inaccessible mountainous areas. The family house, which is also used for drying, is at the bottom of the hill at around 1,400 metres above sea level.

We have seen Pedro’s coffee improve so much that it’s rare to get anything rejected, and we have seen an increase in scores over the three years we have been doing this. We have got to the point where we have a pre-approved volume contract so Pedro can plan for the coming year, and it’s reviewed annually. We now buy nearly 95% of the farm’s coffee, with just 5% being rejected into the Pitalito blend.

The farm is owned and run by all the Claros family: Pedro, his wife Nelcy, and their six children (Alberio, Edilson, Sandra, Hermes, Diana and Monica). It’s a real family business with everyone pitching into the farm to make it work.

NAME: Pedro Claros

AGE: 49

IN COFFEE: 31 yrs

Your proudest achievement in coffee: My biggest accomplishment in coffee is having a person like Stephen from outside of my country interested in my coffee. It makes me very proud to know that he is promoting and commercialising my coffee internationally.

Biggest challenge facing you today: My biggest challenge, which I think is the most common in the industry, is the lack of workforce.

Favourite coffee you've had (not including yours): A coffee from Bruselas in Colombia that's grown by Beto Narvaez.

If you could grow coffee anywhere in the world apart from your own country, where and why: I would like to grow coffee in El Salvador because of all the things I've heard, and what people tell me about that country.

If you had a blank cheque, what would be the one investment you would make in the farm: I would like to invest in the fertilisation, giving my trees better nutrition. I would also like to invest in infrastructure for the farm.

COLOMBIA

Finca Santuario

"Stephen came to Colombia for the first time in 2011. I lived in the States for many years so I have really good English, but when Stephen spoke to me for the first time, I didn't understand a single word. It took me a whole morning to set my mind to his Birmingham accent! Basically I was totally blind for the first hours of his visit ... jajajajaja."

"My favourite varietal is Typica – it has amazing profiles. With the right process you can beat any other varietal. It's given me a lot of awards."

Camilo Merizalde

Camilo is the perfect embodiment of relationships in coffee. Not all relationships are trouble free, and sometimes a lack of communication from both parties can lead to a breakdown in the very thing you're working towards. But thankfully we're very strong now and I'm very happy to be working with him. Camilo has a degree in Economics from the University of South Florida in the United States, which he got in 1990.

After working for an investment company, in around 1995 Camilo began working for a company that used to import food from all over the world. He was charged with sourcing the products from other international businesses. During his travels people would often ask him if he knew companies from Colombia selling good quality coffee. Back then he had thought that his country had the best coffees in the world.

He decided to start learning more about the coffee industry in Colombia. He was able to visit many coffee producing areas and talk to local coops and Federacion de Cafeteros committees.

"I sleep eight hours. I eat healthy. I love dulce de leche. I am ambidextrous. My left eye is set to see close objects, read. My right eye is set for long distances, driving. I run ultra marathons."

By 1998 he could resist it no more and decided to immerse himself in the world of coffee, creating a business plan to develop the best quality farm in Colombia. He chose the Cauca area, and the Santuario farm, which was planted with Bourbon coffee plants, was born by mid 2000.

The farm had an immediate success because Camilo created a farm with the specific needs of the specialty coffee market in mind.

Our story starts back in 2009 when we had been searching for a great Colombian coffee since forever. We found this farm on the offer sheet of an importer we don't usually use, but we bought the coffee because it was tasting great.

We stocked the Typica crop from this farm. It was only a small lot, but it was very popular. The following year we took a bigger lot, which was equally popular.

The coffee and the farm became favourites. But one year we found out from Camilo that the importer would not be bringing in the coffee and all the hard work, searching, and cupping would be wasted. So cue the music and a flight to Colombia (tagged on to the start of my trip to the World Barista Championships).

We bought directly, but some communication issues and shipment problems meant we lost this farm. It was so sad, and I don't think I ever truly forgot this coffee.

Fast forward to Seattle last year and the World Barista Championships (yes, another championship), and I bump into Camilo. After a long conversation, we decided it was for sure worth another try.

Camilo is one of the leading lights in and – you could say – a template for the future of the Colombian coffee industry, with his business approach, vision, and agronomic skill, and some of the most tasty coffee I've ever had from Colombia.

NAME: Camilo Merizalde

AGE: 48

IN COFFEE: 20 yrs

Your biggest influence in coffee: I have had many influences on my coffee career. Hiroyuki Kiriki (who passed away recently, rest in peace) helped me by introducing my coffees to Japan. Also Geoff Watts, who I met in 2003. He became a really good friend who took me by the hand and pulled me around the world of specialty coffees, and still does today.

Your proudest achievement in coffee: The day I sold the first container of coffee to Japan. Also all the awards, which are the recognition of our work in the specialty coffee industry. But also the day that we won the World Barista Championships with Saša Šestić.

Favourite coffee you've had (not including yours): A coffee from Ethiopia, from Hambela farm. It had a blueberry aroma, delicate sweetness, and bright sparkling acidity. I still have it on my mind!

Favourite way to relax: I exercise a lot.

If you had a blank cheque, what would be the one investment you would make in the farm: A community centre with a school, a library, a movie centre and a fitness area.

COLOMBIA

Finca Buena Vista

"In my family, each member has their role. My wife is in charge of preparing food for the pickers, and my brothers work on the processes of beneficios. My father helps me with the transportation to the warehouses when I need to take coffee."

"I became involved in coffee because I come from a coffee growing family. I personally have been working on coffee for almost 20 years."

Edier Perdomo

Edier was born into coffee. He and his family have always been surrounded by coffee trees and coffee processing. Showing great respect for traditional approaches, he questions the conventions and methodologies of coffee growing, pushing the boundaries and breaking the rules – and making delicious coffee.

Sometimes when you're tasting coffee, the world stops. It is almost like a fog comes down, dulling everything and everyone around you. Sounds become muffled and all you can think about is that cupping bowl in front of you.

I can see the cupping of the first time I tasted coffee from Finca Buena Vista in my mind's eye. I'm taken back to exactly the place. It was not only the best coffee on the table, but one of my highlights of the whole trip back in 2013.

I first had Edier's coffee in a blend called Colombia Huila Pitalito Oporapa, which was from eleven different producers; eleven producers who had been picked out on a cupping table as people doing amazing things with coffee. That trip in 2013, cupping the single lots from these producers, gave me my "moment."

"I like to drink a good coffee while I'm relaxing, and invite my friends and neighbours over to give them my coffee to try."

Since then we have gone on to develop and create relationships with three of these eleven. But Edier is the most experimental of them all.

His family own the farm next door to his, and they take a more traditional approach. They are planting rust-resistant varietals like Colombia and Sarchimor, for instance, while Edier perseveres with the vulnerable Caturra because he knows it has a superior cup profile with his set of growing circumstances.

He also does something different at the processing stage. For his fermentation process, Edier fills big blue tanks with 50% wet parchment (just out of the depulper) and then shuts them. He waits for 24 hours before opening the tank again, and then he proceeds with washing the coffee normally. This is an interesting way of fermenting, and I'm convinced this is what makes his coffee so special on the cupping table.

And at that cupping table we make lots of decisions. Cupping individual days' pickings, we approve anything scoring over 86; anything below 86 is rejected, put into a bulk lot (a Pitalito blend) and sold on. Anything over a 90 goes into a special micro lot for which we pay a much higher premium, but it also gives Edier the chance to see what he did with that day's picking and try to replicate what we prize so highly.

But Edier doesn't want to stop here. He wants to invest in lab equipment, like water activity metres and a humidity metre, so he is able to to use these measurements and learn more about what is happening to his coffee at the processing stage before taking it to the warehouse; and so he can improve his coffee year on year.

This is a special relationship from a very special producer who is motivated to do a better job and grow better coffee.

NAME: Edier Perdomo

AGE: 36

IN COFFEE: 20 yrs

Favourite coffee varietal and why: I like Caturra because it's one of the varietals I have in my farm, and it is unique and special because it gives coffee a lot of sweetness.

Your proudest achievement in coffee: My biggest accomplishment in coffee is having the capability to produce high quality coffee, and having clients like Stephen who like my coffee.

Espresso or filter coffee: I like more filter coffee because you can better feel the notes and characteristics of the coffee. In espresso sometimes we can miss those notes that make the coffee special.

Biggest challenge facing you today: My biggest challenge is finding people to work on my farm.

If you could grow coffee anywhere in the world apart from your own country, where and why: I would like to grow coffee in Ecuador because it's a country that's not developed in specialty coffees, so I would like to go there and share my knowledge, good practices, and process on how to produce specialty coffee.

Costa Rica

“The land of the micro mill revolution, where coffee producers have taken full control of the way that they process and market their coffee, which has led to an explosion of different expressions of coffee.”

– Stephen Leighton

C O S T A R I C A

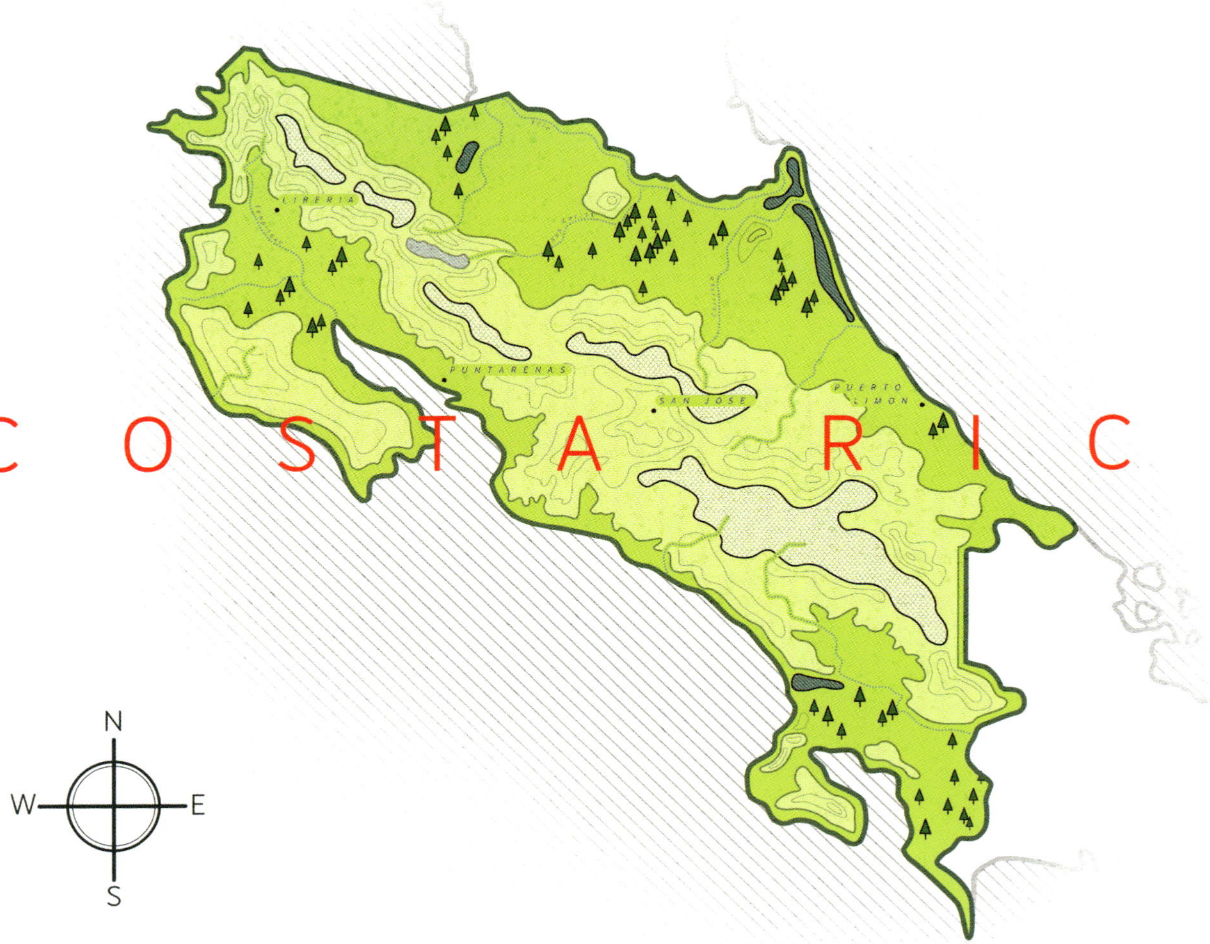

Coffee production in Costa Rica began in 1779, and was introduced during the Spanish colonial rule. Napoleon's occupation of Spain led to the outbreak of revolution all across Spanish America, leading to independence in 1821 and an explosion of coffee production in the region due to tax breaks from the government.

1831 saw law introduced that allowed anyone who planted coffee on unassigned land for five years or more to stake a claim for ownership.

Coffee was vital to the Costa Rican economy by the early-to-mid 20th century. Reliance on coffee and its price fluctuations led to economic difficulties for the country, which resulted in a diversification of its exports and a collapse in the coffee market.

The year 2000 saw a change in the way that coffee producers could process their coffee. Previously they had relied on delivering their cherry to large mills that would mix the coffee into big lots and lose the provenance of the coffee.

But the development of micro mills led to producers taking control of marketing their coffee, introducing more traceability and using innovative processing and cup profiles.

Coffee Facts

Total production in 2016 (60 kg): 1,486,00

Percentage rise and fall on previous year: -9%

Internal consumption in 2016 (60 kg): 436,000

Consumption per capita: 2.76 kg per person per annum

Taste profile: Diverse, but high sweetness and clean cup

Common varietals: Mundo Novo, Villa Sarchi, Bourbon and Geisha

Coffee growing altitudes: 600 m.a.s.l. to 2,100 m.a.s.l.

Rank of coffee production: 15th in the world

Main buyers: USA, Germany the Netherlands, France and England

Unique problems: High cost of living, lack of water for processing, expanding urbanisation

Soil types: Fertile volcanic

Country Facts

Population:
4,905,626 (2017)

Population density:
96 people per km²

Capital city:
San Jose

Land mass:
51,075 km²

Currency:
Costa Rican colón

COSTA RICA

Finca Licho

"From great sacrifices, we have had the joy of seeing the dreams of our family and feeling the benefits of working as a team. The Aguilera Brothers micro mill grows over time and is also a source of work for our families."

"We are a micro benefit, a society currently made up of eight brothers."

Aguilera Brothers

This is a perfect example of a different type of producer. This time it's a micro mill owned by eight brothers who all deliver cherry from their jointly-owned farms to a mill, which they all work. I've been working with them for the past ten years and I've slowly got to meet them all over time, and have got to know them much better on each visit.

I first bought coffee from Finca Licho (one of their many farms) from a Cup of Excellence auction many, many years ago in 2007, where it finished 4th.

Licho is a coffee and relationship that I feel shows our development as a roaster over the years. As I've already said, we first bought this coffee in the Cup of Excellence program (a great way to meet a grower).

Then we bought it from an import broker; they helped us bring in this coffee because we are a small coffee buyer. Then we bought directly from the farm. Then, three years ago, I went out to the farm and did the deal on the farm with the brothers.

"It began in the footsteps of our father, since we were about fifteen years old, helping to sow and work in the crop. With the passage of time and as a result of the joint effort of all the brothers, we're acquiring new lands to dedicate them to the activity that the family is passionate about."

I love the fact that a few years ago I walked onto the farm after cupping a particular lot in the exporter's office, asked how much they wanted, and there was a short conference. They came back and we agreed, we shook hands, and I got back into the 4x4 and drove away.

We continued to develop the relationship to a point where we have now agreed a European-exclusive deal with them for this coffee, and this year.

Each brother has been brought into the business when they hit fifteen years old, learning all the tricks of the trade from their siblings. The oldest brother learnt from his father, who passed on his years of experience of growing amazing coffee. Whilst doing this they have expanded the business, acquiring new farms as they go, pooling their resources to better themselves as a team.

And a team is exactly what they are, regularly playing football together – football being their other passion. It's so much of a passion that when they won the Cup of Excellence competition back in 2007, they took the money and invested in a football pitch for themselves and their workers (and the local community) to use. The best part is that it doubles up as drying patios in the harvest season, when it's difficult to find time to play football.

Every year I've visited I've found that they have done something else, be it building new drying greenhouses, acquiring new farms, or investing in equipment for processing. This year when I visited they were very happy to show me their new varietal garden, where they are planning to experiment with new varieties. They are planting new Geisha, SL 28, Sarchimor, and hybrids, and are also implementing new processes with the honey and natural processes.

A team, a band of brothers, working and playing together, producing exceptional specialty coffee.

NAME: Aguilera Brothers

AGE: Mixed

IN COFFEE: 25 yrs

Your biggest influence in coffee: Our father, who taught us all we know about growing coffee. Even when we were children he would teach us every step of the process.

Your proudest achievement in coffee: The result obtained in Taza de la Excelencia with the coffee of Finca Licho.

Biggest challenge facing you today: Climate change is the biggest factor affecting coffee producers around the world.

Favourite coffee you've had (not including yours): It was a Geisha from Panama. So different to anything we've tasted.

Favourite way to relax: Enjoying football as a family and, of course, sitting down afterwards with a cup of coffee.

If you could grow coffee anywhere in the world apart from your own country, where and why: Costa Rica. It produces the best coffee in the world, and is a country of peace and freedom.

If you had a blank cheque, what would be the one investment you would make in the farm: We would like to invest in eco-tourism (coffee tour) and research.

What makes your coffee special: The love of cultivation, and brothers working together.

Favourite coffee varietal and why: Villa Sarchi, for its production, adaptability to the climate (wind tolerance) and disease resistance.

COSTA RICA

Vista al Valle Finca la Casa

"Our family has been dedicated to coffee production for four generations. Without fear of being mistaken, we have been in this activity for more than 70 years."

“This project we have longed for for years. It is where we become people. Our passion is very strong and dedicated to coffee.”

Oldemar Arrieta Lobo

Oldemar and Marlene Brenes Morera have been in coffee since being left land by Oldemar's grandparents in 2009. For three years they managed to process the coffee using neighbours' equipment, and that's where Oldemar learnt the skills he has today. In 2012 he was able to raise the funds to build his own micro mill and take control of what he was processing.

This was the year I first met Oldemar and Marlene, at the very beginning of their rise to becoming coffee superstars.

The mill is located at 1,550 metres above sea level and is named Vista al Valle. This translates as "view of the valley," and I'm sure you'll understand why if you take a look at some of the pictures on these pages.

They own three farms, the coffee from which is all processed at Vista al Valle. One farm surrounds their mill and home, and is called Finca la Casa; the other two farms are called Zapote and Fidel. Fidel won the Costa Rican Cup of Excellence (CoE) four years ago.

“Our coffee is special because it is produced with great dedication, perseverance and, above all, much love. Leaving aside the cliché, the difference between specialty coffee and a conventional coffee is the work done with a special care.”

On the three farms they work with the varietals Villa Sarchi and Caturra, and choose to focus their process using the honeying method that is very popular in Costa Rica.

Since the CoE result they have sold their coffee to different countries like Japan, Korea, Taiwan, Australia, the USA, Canada and, of course, the United Kingdom.

Each of their farms has a special place in their hearts. Oldemar told me, “since they have their own history that makes them worthy of a different love. For example, the farm La Casa: our grandfather acquired it approximately 65 years ago and there I spent my childhood, adolescence and youth.”

Oldemar said when his grandfather acquired the farm, lots of infrastructure had to be installed. At that time there was no water or electricity, the roads were in poor condition, and the only way to get supplies on the farm or coffee off the farm was by ox and cart.

Marlene and Oldemar have three children (Francisco, Jorge and Marco), who have all inherited a love of coffee. They are closely involved in the process. Oldemar told me: “In this class of companies it is difficult to delimit functions since ‘we all do everything,’ although each one has his preferences in work. For example, the administrative head is Marlene, while in the production part my boys are involved.”

This is a story of perfect timing: taking on processing and raising funds for their own micro mill as they won the Cup of Excellence for Costa Rica meant they had a head start.

It’s also a story of perfect timing for me. Being involved before their door got knocked down by international buyers means we always have a place in the queue for this special coffee, and we have this special relationship because we love the coffee.

NAME: Oldemar Arrieta Lobo

AGE: 56

IN COFFEE: 7 yrs

Your biggest influence in coffee: Our grandparents were definitely the best influence we could have. They instilled in us the values that we still maintain at work and in every activity we carry out day by day.

Your proudest achievement in coffee: In 2013, Finca Fidel was awarded the Presidential Award in Cup of Excellence. This has opened us to the international market, placing us as one of the best coffees in Costa Rica.

What is your favourite coffee varietal and why? Our favourite variety is Villa Sarchí. It has a special complexity when it comes to processing and is always a challenge.

Favourite way to relax: Spending time with my family and my friends is the best way I have to relax.

What's your favourite coffee time of the year: Harvest time. During this season, although the work is doubled, is when the efforts of the year are reflected. Besides that we can employ several people who benefit monetarily during these months, collecting coffee.

If you had a blank cheque, what would be the one investment you would make in the farm: An activity that benefits the community collectively. A business opportunity that allows us to expand and diversify. That way you can give work to more people.

COSTA RICA

ARBAR Finca El Manantial

"Although my children are professionals or are studying whenever they can, they accompany me to the field at harvest time to help me."

Carlos Uriel Arrieta Soto

This coffee started off its life at Has Bean with very little information, even though the producer himself arrived at the cupping soon after I'd tried the coffee.

Much of this was because Carlos had not given the farm and mill a name at that time: it was simply known as Finca Carlos Arrieta. That was in 2013. Now it's 2017, and we know so much more about Carlos, his family and their farms.

I first got to meet Carlos in 2013. It was at the exporter's office on the last day of my visit in Costa Rica. Carlos arrived around ten minutes after I had cupped the first table of coffees, where I had found one lot that was making me sing. I just knew it had to be his coffee.

Here ensued the worst coffee-buying negotiation ever to take place in my career. "How much do you want?" I asked. "How much do you like it?" Carlos asked. "A lot," I replied, to which Carlos said, "I'd like a lot then, please." I said, "OK … "

Luckily at this point a grown-up from the exporter's office stepped in and made sure I didn't give Carlos my house, car and pension plan.

We agreed a price that rewarded Carlos more than he had ever gotten before, and which left me with a home to return to in Stafford. I left with what would turn out as one of our most special coffees, and one of the most special relationships we have in Costa Rica.

"How did I meet Stephen? It was just like the most beautiful experience I have ever had. We arrived at the offices of our exporter, and Stephen cupped several samples of coffee. But one made him very excited, and he immediately told me he wanted our coffee. That was the most exciting moment of our project."

We've since learned there's a mill. It's called Arbar, and is built around their family home. It has drying tables and a small coffee nursery. They didn't have a deplulper, but more about this later. The mill is a 2014 development; before that they would just sell their coffee to the local coop and so have no interaction with the coffee.

Then I found out that they own two small farms. One of them is called El Oasis, and it provided the coffee we bought in 2013. The farm is located in the Western Valley region near to the town of Lourdes de Naranjo. It's 1,600 metres above sea level, and it contains mostly Caturra and a tiny bit of Villa Sarchi. They have plans to plant some micro lots in the future. The farm produces between 700–1,400 kg per year.

The other farm is called Finca El Manantial. It's also in the Western Valley near Lourdes de Naranjo, and is at 1,600 m.a.s.l. It contains mostly Caturra, Catuai and Villa Sarchi.

The farms and micro mill have major input from Carlos, his wife (Maria Isabel), and his children: Yesica, Karen, Estaban and Jose Ignacio.

On my visit to the farm in 2014, Carlos told me how he'd take the cherry to a neighbour to pulp the coffee, and bring it back to his farm to finish the process. This was a huge, time-consuming job. So, on behalf of our customers, I loaned Carlos the money to buy a depulper, and then suggested my customers spend 38p extra per 250g bag that year to repay the loan – and you followed through.

Every year I visit them at the farm (and normally get given a feast). I've even sent our roaster, Roland, to meet them. Every birthday, Christmas, and Easter, and every few weeks, I get emails from them with warm wishes. They're a lovely family. It's an amazing relationship and an even more special coffee, which gets better and better every year.

NAME: Carlos Uriel Arrieta Soto

AGE: 54

IN COFFEE: 54 yrs

Your proudest achievement in coffee: To have been able to export our own coffee specifically to Has Bean. We consider that this has meant a lot of effort of the whole family.

Biggest challenge facing you today: Our biggest challenge is to consolidate our project. We see the need to invest, making improvements in the coffee plantations and in our facilities of the micro mill, but the economic limitations often affect what we want to achieve.

Favourite way to relax: My favourite way to relax is to sit outside my house with a coffee and watch the sunset, and watch the hummingbirds that savour the sugars from the flowers of our garden. That is why our coffee logo for Arbar is hummingbirds flying from flower to flower.

Favourite coffee varietal and why: I bow to the Caturra and Villa Sarchi, which have meant a quality cup in our opinion.

Filter or espresso: We love filter coffee and I think it's because we are accustomed to preparing our own coffee at home – coffee purely handmade, and typical of our customs.

What's your favourite coffee time of the year: All of it! But I love to plant a good and beautiful healthy coffee plant.

COSTA RICA

Don Mayo Finca Bella Vista

"At the age of 20 I was able to alternate my work with study. I worked during the day and studied at night. When I turned 26 I got a nursing degree. I worked in nursing for eleven years – that allowed me to save a little bit of money."

"My dream was to ensure that the care I gave my farms was reflected in the quality of coffee, and to be able to market it directly."

Héctor Bonilla Cruz

Héctor and his family are the model mill and farm for every producer all over the world. Héctor has years of experience and has passed this on to his entire family, who all play a role in the production and marketing process of this coffee. This team approach, and their dedication to quality, is truly impressive.

But this professional approach did not come without lots of hard work. Héctor started with coffee production at a very young age. At just fourteen years old he planted a small quantity of coffee plants on a small piece of land his family owned. He kept it small because he had no means to transport the harvest, so when it was picked he was the one who loaded the plants and, by hand, delivered them to the large cooperative mill where he would get paid for the cherry.

He gradually increased the plants over the next six years, and at the age of twenty he was able to alternate his work with study. He would work during the day and study at night.

“I always remember the way Stephen is dressing at coffee events. It definitely made us laugh, and maybe say ... ‘Stephen is crazy!’”

When he turned 26, he attained a nursing degree from his evening studies. He did nursing until he was 37 years of age; by then he had saved enough money to return full-time to coffee, and dedicated himself solely to growing his coffee plantations and increasing their professionalism.

Héctor put the skills and attention to detail he had learnt in the medical profession to work, and when he turned 40 he took a management position at the Llano Bonito RL Coffee Growers Cooperative just as it was forming. Here he was able to improve his skills of coffee growing, which he did for eight years.

Héctor told me: “During that time, I was worried about learning from the beneficiaries and the commercialisation of the coffee, because I was very attracted to it and passionate.”

Héctor was able to introduce this company to the marketplace and to make many small coffee producers feel like there was stability in coffee production – something that was sadly missing during those times.

Growing in confidence, Héctor realised he was learning more about coffee, its production, and how important it is to grow great coffee and market it professionally.

In 2004 he started his own project, Don Mayo. It was a micro mill where he could process his coffee and use the skills he'd learnt to secure his own and his family's future.

He came 3rd in the Costa Rican Cup of Excellence in 2008, and he bettered that in 2009 by being the overall winner. Other awards include his daughter winning the Costa Rica Barista Championships twice.

It's a family business that acts like a professional outfit, but which has a heart – something I wish I could replicate in Has Bean.

NAME: Héctor Bonilla Cruz

AGE: 66

IN COFFEE: 52 yrs

Your biggest influence in coffee: I do not have one, but many. I have learned from my brothers, friends and many people. Each of the people I have met in my life and that has worked in coffee has helped me to learn and improve.

Your proudest achievement in coffee: What fills me with pride is being a producer of our coffee and having the opportunity to meet my own roaster customers, them being my friends, and having relationships of trust and friendship.

Biggest challenge facing you today: Climatic variations and phytosanitary diseases,

Filter or espresso: I prefer espresso because of its intensity and I like how I perceive the attributes of my coffee. I feel it is like the essence of my coffee.

If you could grow coffee anywhere in the world apart from your own country, where and why: I do not change my country because it has unique characteristics and is very recognised in the world. All origins are special, but I love the coffee that is produced in my region.

If you had a blank cheque, what would be the one investment you would make in the farm: I would invest in aesthetics; ease of working at our mill; improvements for the people who work for us (living conditions); improvements in roads; and better water access.

COSTA RICA

Finca La Pira

"Coffee means life. Over all the days of my life, I spend the nights thinking how I can solve the problems for the next day."

"Experiences have helped me become a better coffee grower, experiences are the things you learn along the way."

Carlos Ureña Ceciliano

Carlos is one of the most interesting characters I've ever met in coffee. He has a curious mind that's always pushing the boundaries of coffee production through cupping every single lot he produces. He is also one of the hardest producers to buy from, because his door is always being banged down by coffee buyers due to his attention to cup quality.

His farm, Finca La Pira, is located in the high altitude Dota Valley of the Tarrazú region. This relatively young estate (for the area) is only 50 years old. Carlos took the farm over from his father when he passed away 21 years ago. In his previous career, Carlos was a cupper for a local cooperative, and his skills were very highly regarded.

We first found this coffee in the Cup of Excellence in 2009, and we are pleased to be reunited with it only recently after a lot of effort and hard work.

After inheriting the family farm, Carlos worked for many years as a certified organic coffee producer because of his strong beliefs of looking after the environmental aspects of the farm.

“We have the problem that, besides the very stony soil, the north winds enter and do not let clouds form. Being dry land where the sun is strong affects the place, and the climatic change is allied against me.”

But he realised doing so was just not possible on this farm. Organic coffee is good, but not possible for everyone. The yield was very, very affected in a negative way. So Carlos looked for alternatives, while still holding the organic principles very close to his heart. For instance, instead of using chemicals to control the weeds, sheep roam freely amongst the coffee plants and eat the weeds (and, strangely, leave the coffee plants alone). They work as automatic and mobile “fertilisation units” (nature’s a wonderful thing). This has eliminated the need for herbicides. This is the kind of thinking Carlos has about coffee.

Whenever I visit the farm, Carlos tells me about how he wakes up in the middle of the night with an idea of how he can better production, change the way the coffee is harvested and processed, or improve on systems. I too suffer from this type of sleep deprivation relating to ideas popping into the head, so I can empathise about it.

During one of these late night bursts of inspiration, Carlos thought that using the coldest water he could would be the best way of processing the cherry. During the night, the Dota Valley gets a really sharp, cold breeze, and it runs through the whole farm. He had noticed the way the water on the mill roof, which sprinkled from processing, was almost frosting over. So he created a sprinkling system and a zinc ramp that the water runs across before hitting the cherries in the fermentation tank. He believes that this almost freezes the mucilage on the coffee seed. He uses the analogy of removing the stone from a plum. If it’s warm, it’s hard to take the flesh away; whereas if it’s cold, it’s much easier to take the mucilage and flesh away from the stone. I am convinced that these little details are what make this coffee so special. I have chased this coffee ever since I first had it many years ago from the Cup of Excellence program. We pay way over the odds for this tiny lot. There is much pestering involved, and many visits to the farm to see Carlos.

But it means both Carlos and I get along. I think he understands now how important this coffee is to me, and how much I appreciate the little things he does to make this coffee special.

NAME: Carlos Ureña Ceciliano

AGE: 61

IN COFFEE: 41 yrs

Your proudest achievement in coffee: When the coffee I have produced is sold with my and the farm's identity.

Biggest challenge facing you today: The climatic changes, the soil's terrain or texture, and the demands of the pickers.

Favourite way to relax: Seeing the places planted with coffee and possible places of planting for the future.

Favourite coffee varietal and why: Caturra, for the ease of planting and yield it gives; but also Geisha, for its lovely floral flavours and cup profile.

Tell us a funny moment working with Stephen, or how you met and the first meeting: When Stephen first bought our coffee, it was through an importer. I was surprised that he was buying all of the coffee I was selling them.

Filter or espresso: I like them both equally.

What makes your coffee special: Simply put: love, passion, climate, height, variety, and handling during processing.

If you could grow coffee anywhere in the world apart from your own country, where and why: In Panama, because the producing area has an excellent climate and volcanic soil.

COSTA RICA

Finca Don Pepe

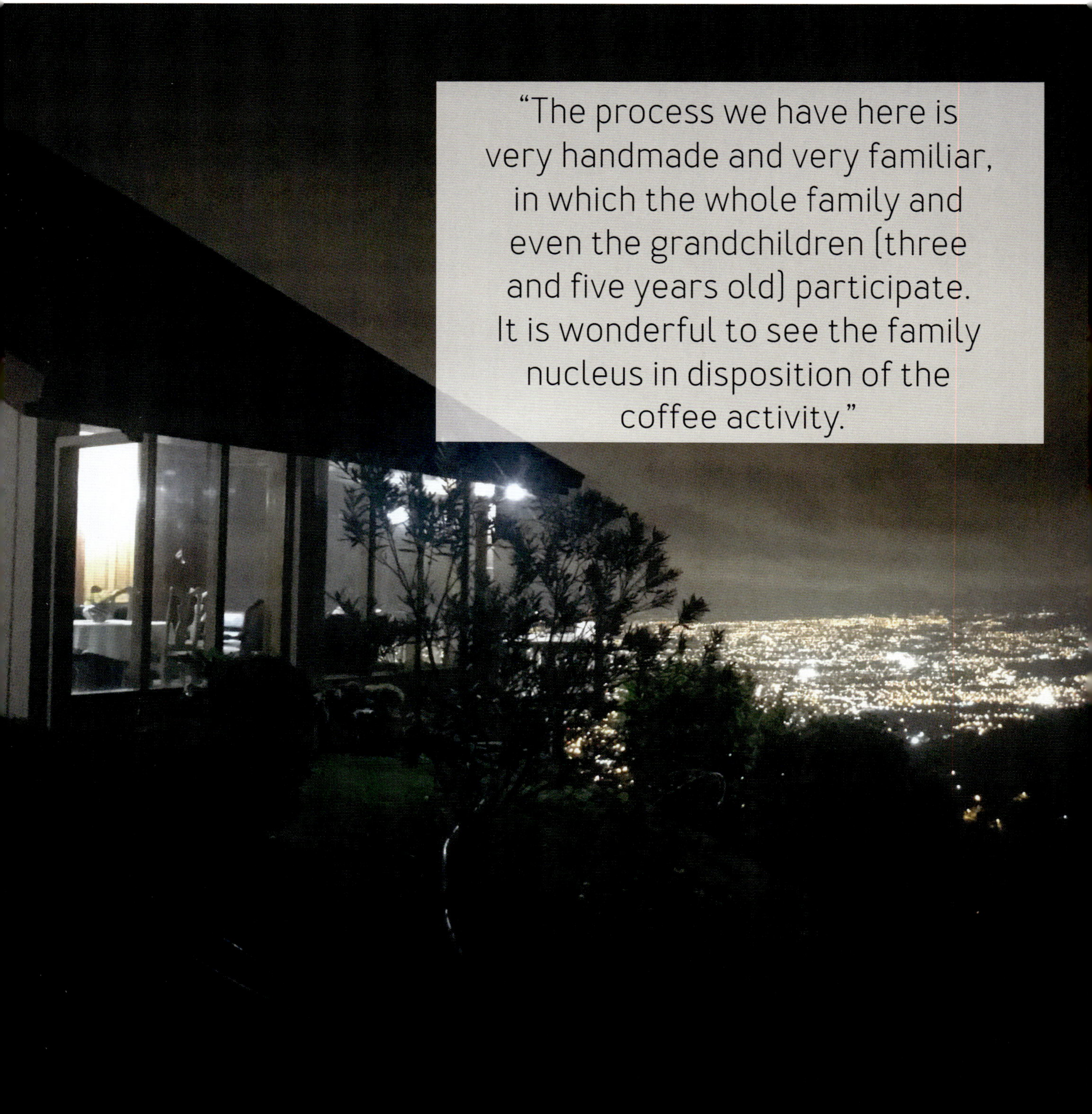

"The process we have here is very handmade and very familiar, in which the whole family and even the grandchildren (three and five years old) participate. It is wonderful to see the family nucleus in disposition of the coffee activity."

"Learning has been very valuable and we have achieved very satisfactory results."

Jose and Daisy Fallas

And now for something completely different. This is a brand new relationship that's in its very infancy: this will be out first year of working together. And it's not just new for us but for anyone, as this is the Fallas' fourth year as coffee producers and they are harvesting their first ever commercial crop. I say "commercial" but this is a real start-up: sorting and processing happens on their dining room table.

It's also a very unusual farm, as you can see from the photos: it's on the very border of the Costa Rican capital city, San José.

I visited them this year in 2017 on the way back from the Tarazzú region. It had been a long day and we had seen many farms, and that evening's dinner was more on my mind than meeting what could be a new coffee and a new relationship.

But I was convinced to go by Joanna Alm and our exporter friend Francisco. And I'm so happy I was convinced, as I got to see this real treat. They live on the farm with their two children and two grandchildren, who are three and five years old, and everyone helps with the production.

> “The farm is at a height of 1,650 metres and the sun covers us from dawn to 2 p.m. This has made Geisha coffee evolve very correctly. For many years we had cows, sheep, goats and horses on the grounds of our farm, and that contributed to the flavour of the soil, which is at its maximum quality.”

Jose told me: “The process we have here is very handmade and very familiar, in which the whole family and even the grandchildren (three and five years old) participate. It is wonderful to see the family nucleus in disposition of the coffee activity.”

They started four years ago after many years of research. They read on the internet about a variety called Geisha. Jose and Daisy spoke to everyone they could and, after many calls, found someone who had the seed for sale.

Geisha seed is very difficult to get hold of, and particularly so the Geisha that the coffee world has come to love. Many producers buy and plant Geisha only to find out that it's not really pure seed, and is either a different varietal or one that has mutated and changed (particularly a problem in Costa Rica).

But at a cupping earlier in the day (before the visit) we had blindly cupped over 100 coffees. One that really stood out and which we all pointed at as Geisha was Daisy and Jose's coffee.

Daisy and Jose had taken this seed they had acquired and planted it on a small piece of land adjoining their family home. For such a young, new and small enterprise, they have already received acclaim.

Last year, in only their third year of production, their coffee was represented in the World Barista Championships 2016 in Dublin, where it received critical acclaim.

This year for the first time we will be showcasing a small lot that we are sharing with Drop Coffee in Stockholm. We are very excited to share it with them, and to ultimately share with you the very newest of our relationships.

NAME: Jose and Daisy Fallas

AGE: 68

IN COFFEE: 4 yrs

Your biggest influence in coffee: Our biggest influence as a producer was Mr Danilo Calvo (R.I.P.), who motivated us to enter this agricultural activity.

Your proudest achievement in coffee: To have had our Geisha chosen to participate in the World Barista Championship in Dublin, Ireland, in 2016.

Biggest challenge facing you today: The greatest challenge has been the knowledge of this very special activity.

Favourite way to relax: The best way to relax is to sit in front of a cup of Geisha coffee watching the mountains we have around.

If you could grow coffee anywhere in the world apart from your own country, where and why: I would choose Costa Rica because it is a beautiful country, which has all the conditions to produce the best coffee in the world.

Espresso or filter coffee: We enjoy both.

What makes your coffee special: Our Geisha is special due to the hand of God that is present in our coffee plantations.

What's your favourite coffee time of the year: The cycles of coffee are so wonderful, we enjoy all these cycles as the coffee flourishes and ripens.

Favourite coffee varietal and why: Our preferred variety is the Geisha for its fruit cup, which is unique.

COSTA RICA

Farami

"One of the most important challenges we have had to face has been to transform our farm into a sustainable farm, the processes for which involve respect and care for the environment; since in the early years it was a conventional farm."

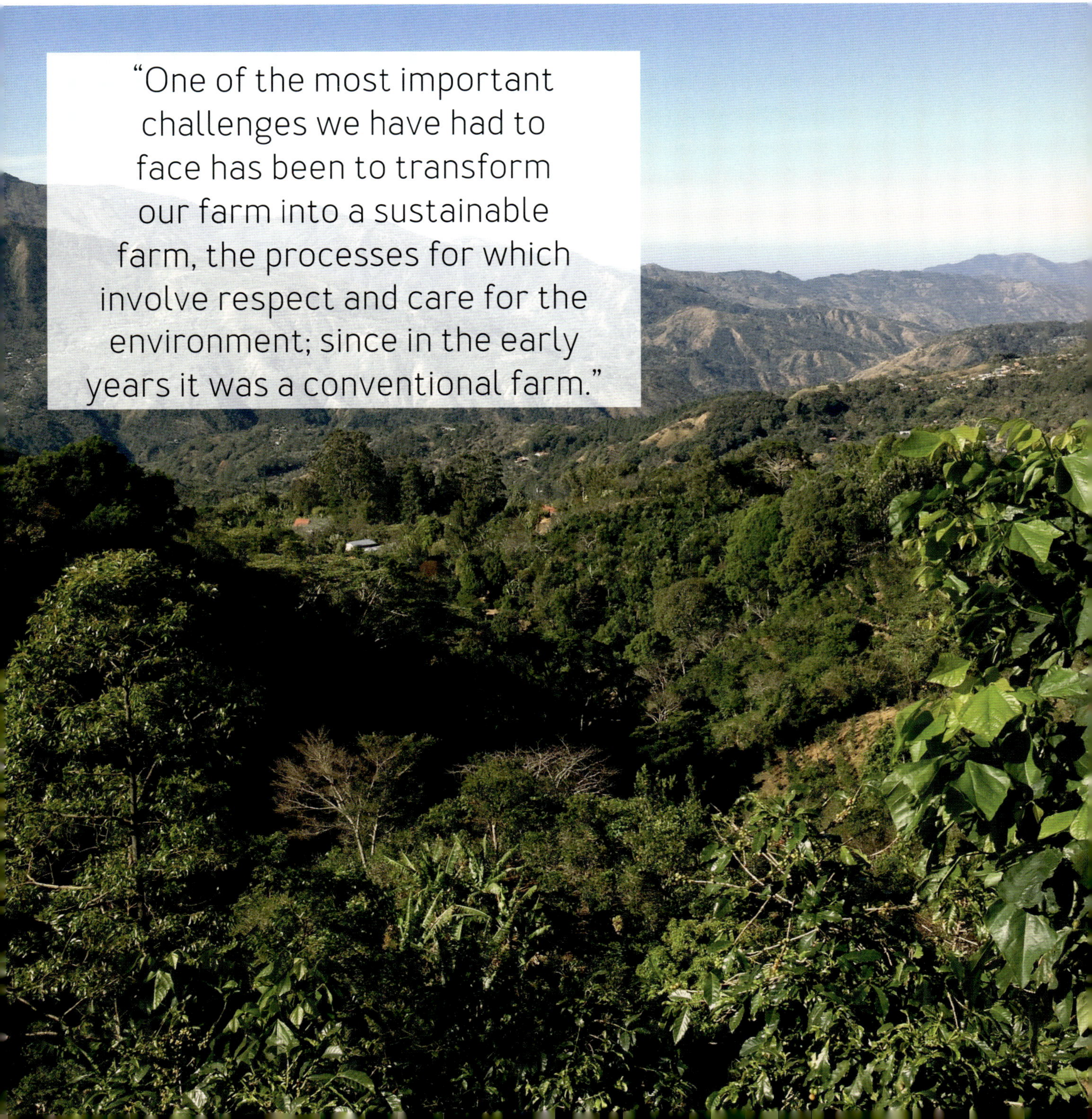

"I love being a coffee producer in Costa Rica because our coffee is the best, because its terrain and conditions are perfect for the production of coffee."

Juan Luis Fallas Mata

This is a coffee producer you may not know if you're a Has Bean customer. I am also a partner in 3FE, which is located in Dublin, Ireland. This is a relationship I look after for them, and it's one of their showpiece coffees. It's also always one of my highlight farm visits, because it's such a unique and different kind of place.

It all started in 1983 when Juan Luis acquired 3.5 hectares of land through a family inheritance. About two years later he started planting coffee plants.

Three years later (as is the way with coffee) the first harvests of coffee began, and he delivered the cherry to the Santa María de Dota cooperative, in Tarrazú de Dota. At the time, this was the normal way coffee producers would do business.

In 2003 Juan Luis's wife, Maria Eugenia Ramirez, inherited 2.5 hectares dedicated to the same production of coffee on neighbouring land, so they decided to pool resources and came together in creating Farami.

“I’m very proud that my farm was awarded the Ecological Blue Flag Award, granted by the Ministry of Agriculture and Livestock, which further strengthens the evidence of the care we seek to give the environment.”

The name of the farm comes from a bit of clever wordplay by them both: Juan Luis Fallas and Maria Eugenia Ramirez, Fallas and Ramírez, Farami … see what they did there? This year they have expanded the farm by buying some neighbouring land to increase their coffee production. They are working towards creating a water power generator, and have installed a lookout tower so the views across the farm can be enjoyed from a vantage point.

In June 2010, their farm was recognised for their environmental responsibility. Because of this they were able to access funding to acquire a micro mill for the pulping process – something that’s very common in Costa Rica, and which was really taking off at that time.

On a visit to Costa Rica in 2011, our exporter Francisco Mena suggested we take a look at this brand new farm he was working with, and so the relationship began.

As an integrated farm, coffee farming is not their only activity. As well as producing coffee, Farami is also a working farm: pigs and chicken and cows are actively farmed side-by-side with the coffee. They’re the farm’s own fertilisation factory. They also use the animal waste for cooking and heating.

Farami doesn’t stop there with its environmental responsibilities. It’s classed as an Integral Didactic Farm, the management of which is friendly with the environment, and it also has good agricultural practices supervised by ICAFE and the Ministry of Agriculture and Livestock.

They have also been awarded the first “Blue Flag” given to a coffee farm in Costa Rica, which is an internationally recognised sign of environmental and sustainability issues being addressed. It is the highest award that can be given to a building or an institution. It’s a special farm run by two special people whom I’m pleased to call friends.

NAME: Juan Luis Fallas Mata

AGE: 50

IN COFFEE: 30 yrs

Your biggest influence in coffee: My grandfather, due to his dedication to everything he did. He was also the first manager of the Dota Coffee Growers Cooperative. He inspired me and made me fall in love with producing coffee.

Your proudest achievement in coffee: Positioning our coffee in the international markets and obtaining the third place in the Cup of Excellence 2013.

Biggest challenge facing you today: Climate change.

Favourite coffee you've had (not including yours): La Pira de Dota grown by one of our neighbours, Carlos Ureña Ceciliano.

Favourite way to relax: Feed the farm animals and play sports.

Favourite coffee varietal and why: My preferred variety is Bourbon because of its fruity cup.

What's your favourite coffee time of the year: Harvest time. This is because it is when the cherry is ripe and its aroma on the farm is good.

Tell us a little about your family and how they are involved: Our family is made up of four members: my wife, my daughter, my son-in-law and I. We are very united, we make decisions together, and we share the same passion for coffee and the farm.

COSTA RICA

Finca Sumava de Lourdes

"I became involved in coffee 25 years ago, working for an exporting and milling company in Costa Rica. It definitely became an encounter with passion, with something I found a purpose to work in."

"I'm most proud of being part of and collaborating with Costa Rica's Micro Mill Revolution."

Francisco Mena

Francisco is a force of nature. Coming from working in the commodity market within Costa Rica, he has single-handedly raised the profile of Costa Rican micro mill speciality coffee forever by relentlessly pushing the boundaries of what was possible in the coffee market of Costa Rica. Exporter and now farmer, his journey is one of the most interesting.

Beginning in the early '90s, Francisco worked for an exporting and milling company in San José, Costa Rica. A long way from where he is now, he saw the dawn of a revolution in which he would be a major player.

Founding his own export company, Exclusive Coffees, in 2008 with his friend and business partner Juan Ramon, he set about adding some previously lost identity to the amazing coffees that had been hidden for so many years in huge lots of Costa Rican SHB and Tarrazus, which the big mills had cornered for so long.

He had to find both customers and suppliers. But the market was just beginning with the advent of small, affordable micro mills in reach of small producers.

These small producers moved away from processing their cherries at larger mills and toward building micro mills on their farms. This allowed them tighter control over the processing stage of their coffee, which led to better quality. It also gave them increased economic viability and the traceability that specialty coffee buyers crave.

But without a route to market, many of these producers didn't have anywhere to sell their coffees. Enter Francisco and Juan Ramon, who built the perfect storm to launch Costa Rican coffees upon the world.

"I have learned on this beautiful coffee journey that moments and events happen one step at a time, and we must appreciate each one of them as a learning treasure."

My first visit with Francisco was a crazy two days during which we visited thirty farms, and the beginning of what is a very special friendship. The one thing that struck me was that anything was possible. "Can we separate these varietals?" Was answered with "yes, of course." "Can we do some different honey projects?" Was also met with "yes, of course." It's the mantra of these amazing partners.

But this is a book of coffee producers, and two years ago Francisco was presented with the opportunity to become a partner in a new farm venture called Sumava de Lourdes. He put into practice all the ideas he had been sharing with producers. I remember a conversation with him where he told me that some old-school producers would dismiss his ideas because "he was not a coffee producer."

In just under a year after taking over the farm, Sumava de Lourdes was entered into the Cup of Excellence program in Costa Rica and came in first place, on their first time entering any competition. I guess he has the perfect reply to their doubt now: he can just show them his trophy. He's a true coffee giant, and a true friend.

NAME: Francisco Mena

AGE: 46

IN COFFEE: 25 yrs

Favourite coffee varietal and why: For quality, resistance and productivity: Villa Sarchi. Regarding complexity and exoticness: recently we experienced a new species called Sessiliflora. This species will break all rules!

Biggest challenge facing you today: Sudden climatic changes that favour fungus, rust, and all kinds of plagues.

Favourite way to relax: Sharing time with my wife and two children, Alessia (13) and Emma (9), at the farm, Sumava.

Tell us a funny moment working with Stephen, or how you met and the first meeting: Many years ago we met in Costa Rica, in his first trip I believe. His personality makes him different and you need to get to know him well to understand the great person he is.

If you could grow coffee anywhere in the world apart from your own country, where and why: I love Costa Rica.

Espresso or filter coffee?: Filter every time.

If you had a blank cheque, what would be the one investment you would make in the farm: I'd love to invest in a state-of-the-art childcare centre.

What makes your coffee special: Care, passion, dedication and terroir.

Favourite coffee you've had (not including yours): Kenyan.

COSTA RICA

Don Joel San Luis
Finca La Cumbre

"[The first years were] a challenge because the farm was in very bad condition and without harvest. I had to increase my effort in the day with working the farm, and at night I was going to work driving a taxi just to be able to carry on the expenses."

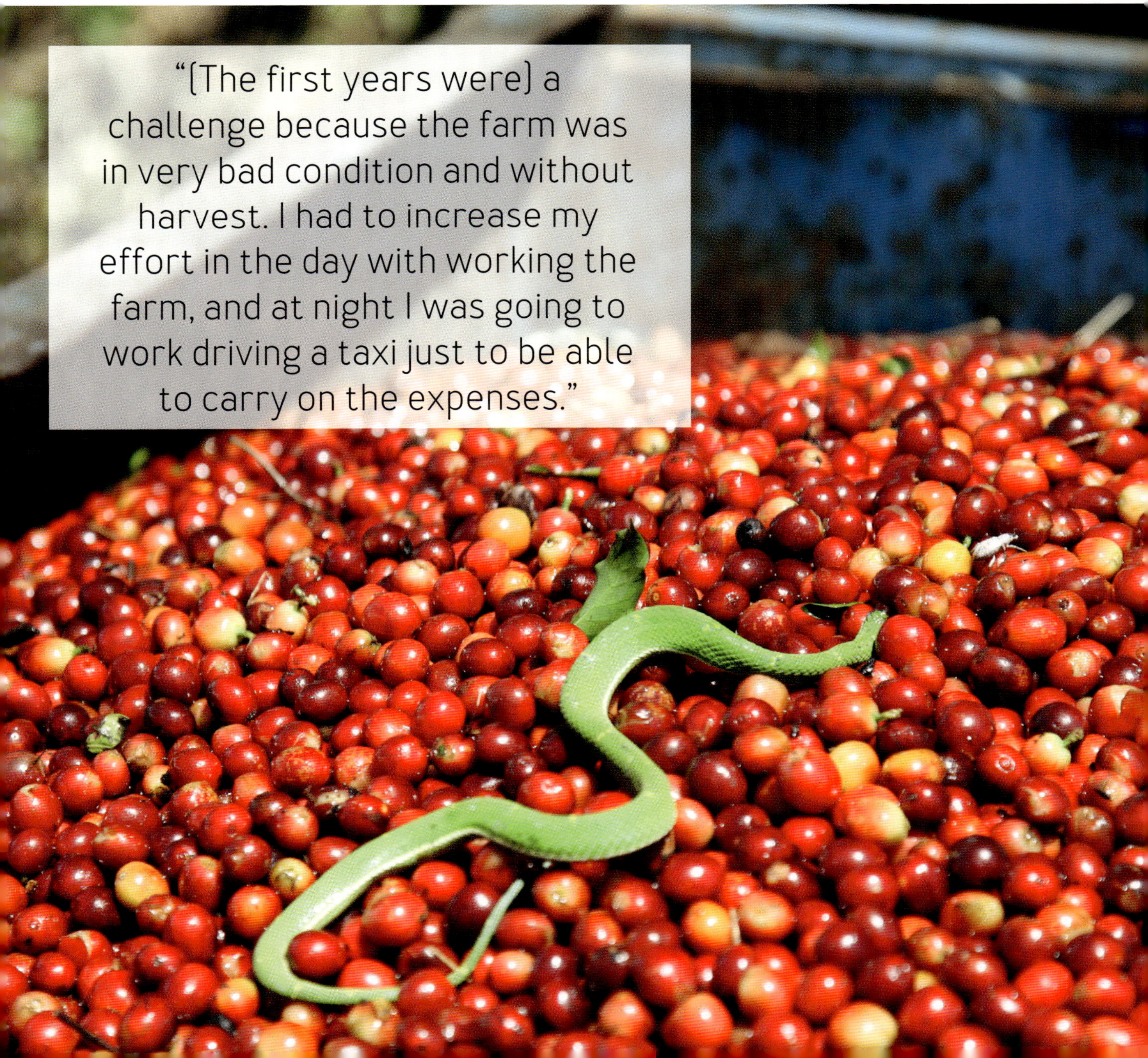

"Since I was a child, I participated in the activity with my father along with my brothers; we did it in a traditional way."

Allan Oviedo Rodriguez

Allan is someone I've worked with for as long as I've worked in Costa Rica. Honest, hard working, friendly and willing to try anything are the things I most associate when I think of Allan.

His whole life has been dedicated to growing amazing coffee, and with much success. Over the six years of our working together, he's become a very important partner.

Allan's farm is called Finca La Cumbre and is in the San Luis de Grecia area of the Central Valley, on the edges of the capital city San José. Allan is a second generation grower. Although he officially took over from his father, Don Joel, twelve years ago when Don passed away, Allan has worked on the farm his whole life.

Don Joel's name lives on though; Allan named the micro mill after his father. Allan is married with two children: a ten-year-old boy and a five-year-old girl.

Allan has participated in the farm since he was a child, working with his father and his brothers.

> "I wanted something different for me. This started with the micro mill. It was a very difficult experience as I did not have the resources to invest in infrastructure or the knowledge."

Growing coffee like everyone else, they did it in a traditional way of Costa Rica, taking all the production to the cooperative of the area whereupon they were paid for the cherry. It was the last interaction the farm would have with the coffee.

After his father's death in 2001, the farms were divided between the brothers, and Allan kept producing in the same traditional way he had always done.

Allan told me: "The first years were very hard because the farm was in a very bad condition, with 80% of the crop being the Catimor variety. The problem with the Costa Rica Catimor is it is not good in the cup. Also many of the plants were more than 25 years of age, which decreases yield and quality. We also suffered with the leaf fungus Ojo de Gallo, or 'The eye of rooster.' Added to this, at the beginning of the summer there were strong winds that finished destroying the plantation. But I saw the land of the farm was good, just with few resources.

That year was a challenge because the farm was in very bad condition and without harvest. I had to increase my effort in the day with working the farm, and at night I was going to work driving a taxi just to be able to carry on the expenses."

To fix this problem Allan started the huge task of not only changing the plant stock, but also installing a micro mill. But this added to the problems because Allan had little experience processing, and had a very steep learning curve.

Allan told me, "I remember the first week that the micro mill was operational. I went to ask the processing manager of CoopeVictoria to explain how I could know when the coffee was ready. Luckily he taught me the basics, and I learnt as I went along."

Allan is normally the first person you meet when landing in Costa Rica as his is one of the first farms on the way into the Central Valley. It's a good thing; I always leave his farm full of optimism and happy to have caught up with a good friend.

NAME: Allan Oviedo Rodriguez

AGE: 39

IN COFFEE: 34 yrs

Your biggest influence in coffee: My father, who taught me all I know.

Your proudest achievement in coffee: To be able to see the farm in good conditions and to produce good quality coffee.

Biggest challenge facing you today: Trying to grow in production yields without affecting quality of the cup.

Favourite way to relax: Walking absolutely anywhere with my family. We enjoy long walks.

If you could grow coffee anywhere in the world apart from your own country, where and why: I do not know much about coffee production in other countries, but I would not choose anywhere other than Costa Rica – although it is very expensive to produce here.

What's your favourite coffee time of the year: The days of flowering make me feel the aroma so that, when walking through the coffee plantations, it makes me not want to return home soon.

Tell us a funny moment working with Stephen, or how you met and the first meeting: I remember the time I met Stephen. I saw something at the root of a coffee plant. I put my hand down and found a snake. I gave it to him with a knife but he didn't want it, so I put it on the coffee. It was totally green and stood out a lot between the red cherries.

El Salvador

"Sometimes you can't put your finger on why you feel at home somewhere, but El Salvador ticks all the boxes for me and feels like my second home."

– Stephen Leighton

EL SALVADOR

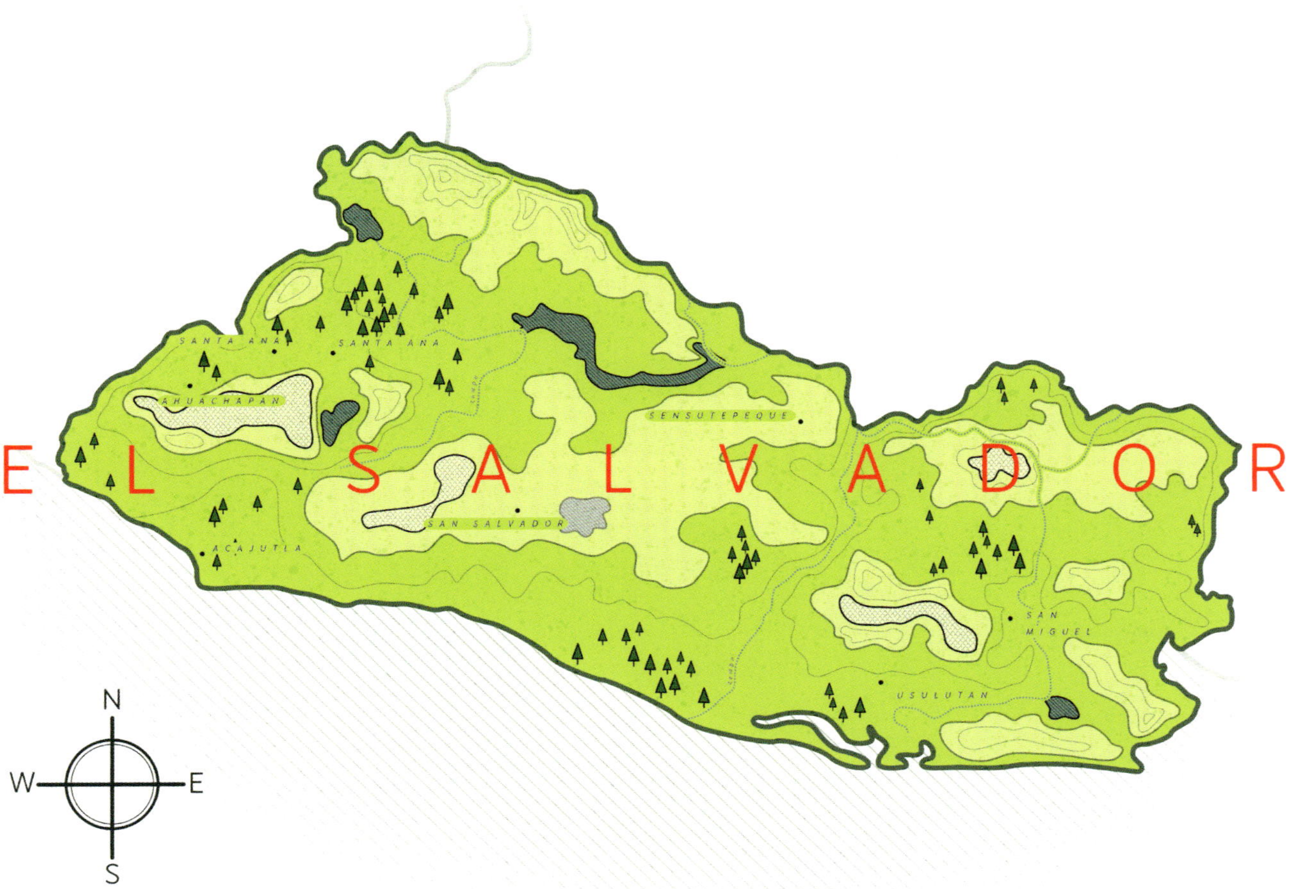

I first visited El Salvador in 2007, and every year since I have returned – not because I have to, but because I want to. Over the years I have seen the political situation and safety in the country decline, but there is something about the people that draws you in.

I have also made the most friends here; not just coffee friends, but real, true friends whom I call for a chat as well as to see how the harvest is getting on.

The country has had its coffee growing challenges: the rise in gang culture, but more devastating has been the attack of a fungal disease called leaf rust. It appears as a small orange dusty mark on the leaves of the coffee plant and spreads from plant to plant if untreated. This makes the leaf die and fall off, stopping photosynthesis and ultimately killing the plant if it remains untreated. It can't be cured but can be managed, yet yields have suffered dramatically in El Salvador because its majority varietal Bourbon is more susceptible to the disease.

In spite of these challenges, to me El Salvador still produces some of the best coffee in the world, and has some of the warmest and hardest working people I have ever met. It also feels like home.

Coffee Facts

Total production in 2016 (60 kg): 623,000

Percentage rise and fall on previous year: +12.9%

Internal consumption in 2016 (60 kg): 275,000

Consumption per capita: 2.7 kg per person per annum

Taste profile: Sweet, balanced and gentle acidity

Common varietals: Bourbon, Pacamara and Pacas

Coffee growing altitudes: 500 m.a.s.l. to 1,900 m.a.s.l.

Rank of coffee production: 19th in the world

Main buyers: USA, Germany, United Kingdom

Unique problems: Leaf rust, un-diverse varietal stock, rural gang issues

Soil types: Volcanic alluvium

Country Facts

Population:
6,167,147 (2017)

Population density:
298 people per km^2

Capital city:
San Salvador

Land mass:
20,723 km^2

Currency:
US dollar

EL SALVADOR

Finca Noruega

"It makes me so proud to be amongst the top specialty coffees in El Salvador."

"In one of Stephen's visits to our farm, La Fany, a couple of years ago, he decided he wanted a picture of him climbed in one of the shade trees, but in the process of climbing he ripped his pants."

Carmen Elena Esteves de Silva

I first met Carmen back in 2006, whilst on an origin trip with an importer which took in El Salvador and Nicaragua.

But I first tasted one of her farm's coffees back in 2003 when we first bought from Finca La Fany; it was one of the first coffees that we had in our portfolio. Since then, Carmen and her husband Rafael have become very good friends.

Carmen married her husband Rafael 30 years ago, and very quickly learnt about coffee farming. He is a fifth generation coffee grower and it's in his veins, passed from father to son; but Carmen found that living with someone who is so dedicated to quality coffee production fuelled her own passion for coffee.

Not only bringing up her family, Carmen plays an essential role in the marketing and back office, and is a vital link between the buyer and her husband, the technician. Carmen's children also play an important role in the farms.

> "Not only bringing up her family, Carmen plays an essential role in the marketing and back office, and is a vital link between the buyer and her husband, the technician."

Her oldest son, Rafael Gerardo, works in the business after learning some important skills as a planner for Siman (a department store in Central / South America). Rafael Gerardo is working as his dad's right-hand man, and learning the skills that Rafael learnt from his father before that.

Rodrigo, their second son, has been working with them for the past four years. He helps with marketing whilst continuing his studies in the USA. He is a frequent visitor home and helps remotely. Valeria, their youngest daughter, is in charge of media and branding, and has been behind professionalising their social media outlets – Instagram in particular.

Coffee is simply not just growing and processing: if you want to be the very best, you also have to market; support your buyers with regular updates and arranging visits; do the exporting; and complete the financial back office duties of invoicing and accounting.

This team approach is what makes Sicafe a leading light in El Salvadorian coffees.

They have a number of farms: Finca La Fany, Finca La Siberia, Finca Noruega, Finca Llano Grande, Finca San Cayetano, and Finca La Divina Providencia.

They also invested in a mill, San Pedro, in 2010. This was not to save money, but so Rafael could have all the control he wanted. Rafael is a control freak, and that's why having his family be strong parts of the business is important – so he surrounds himself with people he can trust to cover the weaknesses in his skill set.

They were winners of a Cup of Excellence award in 2005 for La Fany; in 2005, 2007, 2008 and 2012 for La Siberia; and in 2010 and 2012 for Llano Grande.

Carmen is also particularly proud of the AVPA award for their roasted coffee. They got the Silver Medal Award for gourmet roasted coffee 2016 from the Agence Pour la Valorisation des Produits Agricoles, Paris, France, in 2017.

NAME: Carmen Elena Esteves de Silva

AGE: 61

IN COFFEE: 30 yrs

Your biggest influence in coffee: This is my husband, Rafael Silva.

Your favourite coffee varietal and why: Pacamara variety is my favourite because it has everything you would want in a cup: acidity, complexity, body, and aroma.

Biggest challenge facing you today: Climate change, government policies, diseases and the absence of labour.

Espresso or filter coffee: This has to be filter coffee. I like to sit down, enjoy and relax with my coffee.

If you could grow coffee anywhere in the world apart from your own country, where and why: in Colombia (Eje Cafetero). I fell in love with the surroundings, vegetation, and rich soils, and its people.

What is your favourite time of the coffee year: During the harvest, which brings tradition, colour and joy into the farms.

Favourite coffee that isn't yours: Organic Hama from Ethiopia.

EL SALVADOR

Finca La Fany

"I'm incredibly proud of our achievements that we have received high acclaim for. So many prizes and recognitions in all the different farms in competitions, such as Cup of Excellence."

"My favourite coffee time of year has to be the joy of the harvest."

Rafael Enrique Silva Hoff

Every coffee farmer works hard – it goes with the territory – but Rafael is the most hard working I've ever seen. He runs a number of farms (Finca La Fany, Finca La Siberia, Finca Noruega, Finca Llano Grande, Finca San Cayetano, and Finca La Divina Providencia) and his own mill … there are not enough hours in the day.

Rafael's long-suffering business partner and wife Carmen recalled a story to me about Christmas Day: Rafael turned up at 8 p.m. in the evening on Christmas Eve to celebrate the traditional Christmas, and by 7 a.m. was back in the truck heading to Apaneca to the mill, to get back to work and continue processing the incoming harvest. I think it's fair to call Rafael a control freak, and to say he's obsessed with all the details of picking and coffee processing.

Rafael started very young when his father, Luis Silva, took him along with him to the farms whenever he visited them. Each time Rafael got involved more and more, learning and soaking up all his knowledge from working on the farms.

At an early age he was introduced to the different facets of coffee, cultivars, and agronomic information he had learnt from the previous generation.

When he reached his 21st birthday, his father gave him a present. It was not your normal keepsake for your 21st, but a coffee farm in the shape of Finca Siberia. He told Rafael to work it.

Since that day he's kept building his own knowledge, continuing to use his father's experience but adding his own mechanical common sense approach to farming. If there isn't a tool to do the job he wants, Rafael builds it or fabricates it; that's the kind of man he is.

"I first met Stephen in 2006. He came with a group of European buyers from several countries, but he stood out from the rest because of his happy nature."

It's very much a family business with Rafael's wife Carmen (also in this book) and his oldest son, Rafael Gerardo. Rodrigo, their second son, is also involved, and their daughter Valeria is in charge of branding and social media.

I've been buying from the family now for over fourteen years, and their coffees are staples of many of our most loyal customers. Life without Finca La Fany just doesn't sound like much fun at all.

One of my fondest memories of Rafael was a few years into buying from the family, and I was stopping at their home in Apaneca. We knew each other well, but it's fair to say I ended up spending more time with Carmen, who is the more fluent English speaker and looks after guests while Rafael is processing the coffee. Rafael speaks great English but doesn't always feel so confident about it, but one night he said "come on, let's go for rum."

A night in Apaneca with both him and Carmen, eating pupusas (a traditional Salvadoran dish made of a thick, handmade corn tortilla with fillings) at – from what I'm told – the best pupusería in the world, drinking good rum, remains one of the best nights out I've ever had ... even if the memory is a little hazy thanks to the rum.

NAME: Rafael Enrique Silva Hoff

AGE: 63

IN COFFEE: 42 yrs

Your biggest influence in coffee: My father, for all the tradition he passed to me from the generations of knowledge and practices of our family.

Your proudest achievement in coffee: Being able to pass the same passion that I have for the farms to my children.

Favourite coffee varietal and why: Pacamara, because it has body, dark chocolate flavours and acidity like green apples and grapes. My favourite.

Favourite way to relax: Enjoying nature while I walk around the coffee trees.

If you could grow coffee anywhere in the world apart from your own country, where and why: It has to be El Salvador because it's a small agricultural country with good hand labour.

Tell us a funny moment working with Stephen, or how you met and the first meeting: We had much fun when he came to the mill a couple of years ago and interviewed us for his In My Mug. We have known Stephen for many years and we cherish his friendship.

EL SALVADOR

Finca La Gloria

"My mum is a fourth generation coffee grower. My son loves to visit the farms, and I'm glad he will probably follow our steps and become a coffee grower. My husband I met through coffee, and we are always surrounded by it."

"My favourite time of the coffee year is when the trees are blossoming, no doubt."

Maria Jose Huezo

Maria Jose is a very special lady. But it's no surprise when you realise she is the daughter of the amazing Gloria Rodriguez of Finca San Jose. With a role model like that in your life, you're always going to be a special person. But when you also bring her husband Luis into the equation ... well, this family is special.

Surrounded by coffee all her life, Maria Jose recalls summers with her grandparents in Ahuachapán. She tells me of times when she was working with her grandfather all summer. They would leave the house at 4 a.m. to visit the farms, and plan out what work needed to be done for the day.

Maria Jose tells me with a huge smile on her face that these are her most cherished memories from her childhood.

But the civil war in El Salvador made Ahuachapán a dangerous place, and the visits to her grandfather and the farms were no longer possible. The civil war is so fresh in the minds of many young Salvadorans, and the effect it had on Maria Jose was that she fell out of love with the countryside.

“I met Steve after the awards ceremony for CoE in 2009. He wasn’t part of the jury that year but was visiting, and I remember his smile and sense of humour. I remember his red shoes and cool attitude. We were on a bus the next day to visit the winning farm. He was so excited. I love the joy he brings to simple stuff.”

Maria Jose went on and studied in San Salvador, and became disconnected from her countryside roots.

In 2007 Gloria Rodriguez (her mother) had become more and more interested in raising the quality of her farms after seeing an emerging speciality market become interested in paying more money for better coffee. Gloria decided to enter the Cup of Excellence competition, and placed 10th overall in the coffee in El Salvador that year.

Maria Jose joined her for the award ceremony and was amazed at the international interest in coffee. Realising the potential not only of the family farms, but of coffee in El Salvador, she became more involved.

In 2008 there was an opportunity for her to start working in the Consejo (the Salvadoran Coffee Council), and a year later an opportunity for her to work as the Cup of Excellence National Coordinator.

She went on to buy a farm with her husband Luis, which they called Finca La Gloria – taking inspiration for the farm name from her mother. She told me: “Coffee is a matter of heritage for me, and I feel it in my blood. I have learnt that even if it’s a tough job, it is very rewarding and there is no place to feel at peace like the mountains in Apaneca.”

For someone so young, she has crammed a lot into her life. She’s a coffee producer and a mother, and more recently she took on a battle against cancer. This meant she had to go to the United States of America for medical treatment; that took her away from her beloved El Salvador and farm, but most importantly from her family. Through the power of the internet – how I came to meet Maria Jose and her husband Luis – I followed the treatment on Facebook, and felt so close and involved on her recovery journey.

With her faith and fight, she is now on the road to recovery, and back producing amazing coffee.

NAME: Maria Jose Huezo

AGE: 36

IN COFFEE: 8 yrs

Your biggest influence in coffee: This has to be my grandfather, José María Rodríguez.

Your proudest achievement in coffee: After working in the program, being awarded with a spot in Cup of Excellence. Standing up to get that diploma was priceless.

Biggest challenge facing you today: Balancing work as an employee to sustain my livelihood and the time we need to invest in producing the best coffee we can on the farm. It is a tough balance.

Favourite way to relax: Music. I like to sing. I also like meditation and getting some time off watching the stars, and playing with my son.

If you could grow coffee anywhere in the world apart from your own country, where and why: I would love to experience Africa, it would be such an adventure to understand the culture. I've never been.

If you had a blank cheque, what would be the one investment you would make in the farm: Build our own mill and process our own coffee.

EL SALVADOR

Finca Argentina

"I love it right after the harvest, when we can start to plan ahead for the next year and all my friends in coffee pay us a visit."

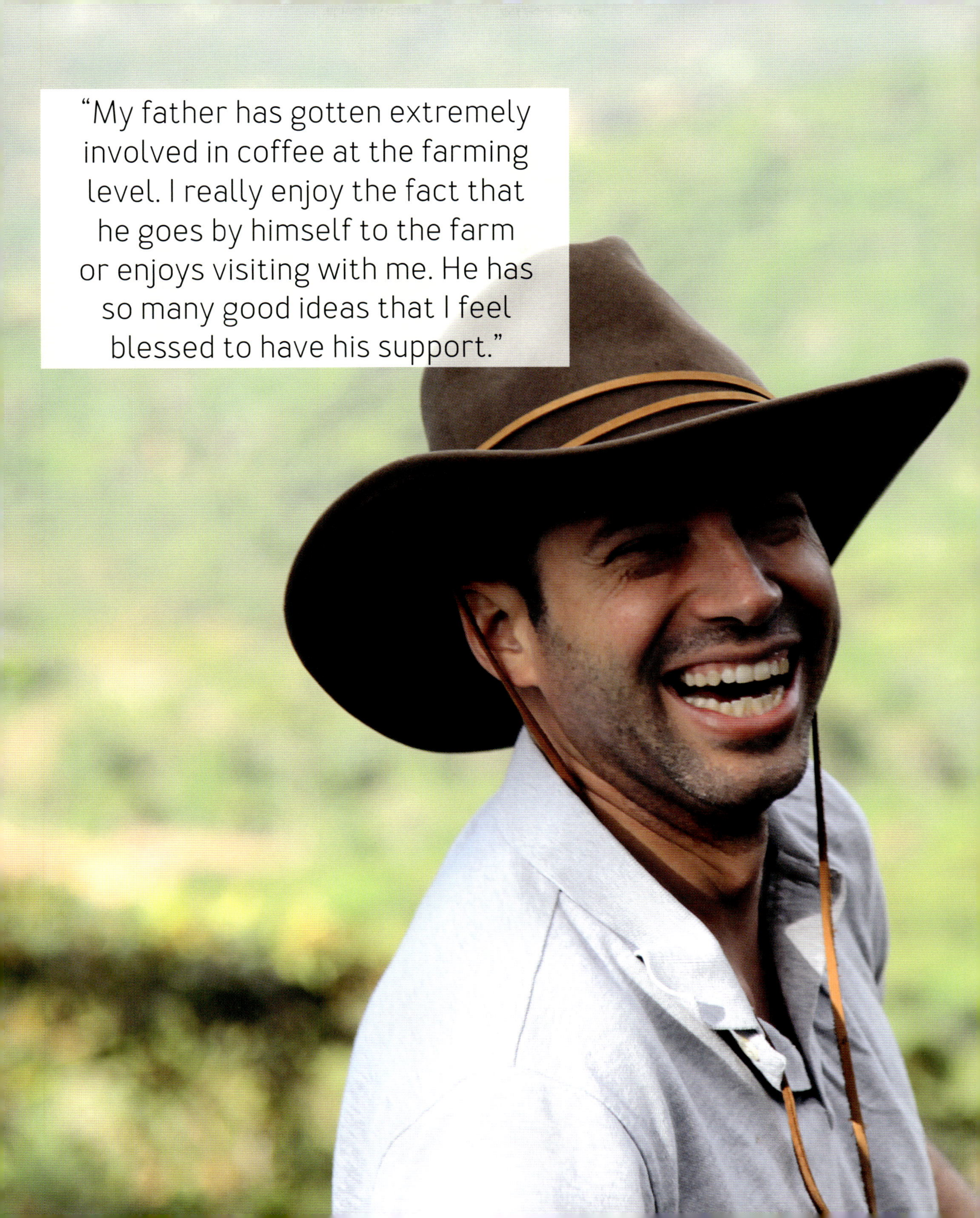

"My father has gotten extremely involved in coffee at the farming level. I really enjoy the fact that he goes by himself to the farm or enjoys visiting with me. He has so many good ideas that I feel blessed to have his support."

Alejandro Martinez

This chapter feels kind of strange to write. I'm not sure how you write an objective review of the relationship you have with your best friend. You see, over the years Ale (yes, easier than Alejandro) has become one of my closest, if not the closest friend I have, and it's all because of a coffee sample seven years ago.

Ale became involved in coffee just eight years ago. At that time he had just relocated to El Salvador from New York, where he had worked as a city banker.

While looking for work in El Salvador, Ale decided to help his father with some of his business interests and investments.

His father had inherited several coffee farms from his grandfather and was unsure what to do with them. His father himself had relocated to El Salvador from Costa Rica just a few years before Ale, and he was not really sure what to do with the properties. Going through their details, one farm stood out as interesting.

"I used to relax by going down to the beach to surf for a few hours. Now, the crowds just make that activity quite the opposite of relaxing. Thus, I relax nowadays by spending as much time as I can at the farm. It is just so peaceful: no cell phone reception, great views, cooler weather – the works."

They had this one farm called Finca Argentina that, unlike others, was solely owned by his father (other farms were co-owned with his father's brother). Ale told his father to let him assess the situation before they took any decision, and visited Finca Argentina.

He only spent a few hours on that first visit, but he did spend some time with Don Victor, a 68-year-old man who had been hired by his grandfather the year Ale was born.

Don Victor talked about the good old days when the farm produced twice as much coffee. Don Victor was Finca Argentina's mandador, which is basically like a foreman. Through him, Ale procured some historical records on the farm's production. He had kept detailed records of the farm yields in a scrappy notebook for over 30 years. Ale has told me that were it not for those records, it is likely he would have sold the farm back then.

Those records showed that Finca Argentina, with only 35 hectares, used to generate more than 800 bags of green coffee per year. The historical record year in the mid-nineties produced 1,300 bags. For the last decade or so, the farm had only produced about 400 bags. It seemed obvious that Finca Argentina only needed proper supervision and adequate investment in order to increase production to acceptable levels.

This is where I entered the stage. Ale found out that the farm had been classified for a Q auction back in 2005. Thinking there may be a specialty buyer out there, he and his cousin (who lived in London) went about sending samples to coffee roasters anywhere they could. We get a lot of these, but unusually I liked this coffee and the rest is history.

Since then Finca Argentina has gone from strength to strength, but not without bumps in the road. In 2013 it suffered the worst harvest on record, with only 70 bags harvested. The loss was approximately 90% of the previous year's yield. But with investment and hard work, they have also bought a neighbouring farm and the future is amazingly bright for Ale and his father.

NAME: Alejandro Martinez

AGE: 41

IN COFFEE: 8 yrs

Your biggest influence in coffee: A fellow farmer and friend, Emilio Lopez. He opened my eyes to all the possibilities of coffee with processing and farming. That interaction motivated me to make changes at the farm and to travel and visit other producers.

Your proudest achievement in coffee: Not sure I have something. I feel there is so much I could do and so many things that are still "work in progress." Ask me again in five years.

If you could grow coffee anywhere in the world apart from your own country, where and why: I love Nicaragua. The country is just beautiful and the people are extremely friendly. I would love to own a farm there.

Favourite coffee varietal and why: Moka. I finally harvested some Moka this year and I loved it. The cup was fantastic. The varietal really shines through and nothing at Finca Argentina tastes quite like it. Plus, the small size makes the beans bizarre to behold.

EL SALVADOR

Finca La Ilusión

"I am married to Maria Alicia Menendez and we have two children, Mariana Florencia and Sebastian Alejandro. I have been married seventeen years, and my life revolves around coffee and my family."

"I can only say thanks, thanks, thanks to God for giving me the opportunity in my life to know, produce and work with this wonderful coffee bean."

Ernesto Menendez

I feel like I have grown up with this man. We both found ourselves in the middle of speciality coffee around the same time, were around the same age, and we both love cupping coffee. Ernesto is more than just a producer: he is a friend, and he is also the first person who really trusted me to showcase his coffee.

Ernesto began his involvement in coffee after his father died in 1995. He inherited the farm and mill, Finca San Carlos. But at just nineteen years old, it was a huge life change for him. Just a couple of years into his studies, he had to leave university to learn from the very beginning about coffee farming, and how to process and operate a working coffee farm.

To further his knowledge, in 1999 Ernesto began to work for James Hill Company, a well-known, experienced coffee mill in Santa Ana city. He began in the informatics and coffee quality control areas. This is where he learnt to love cupping. For a year he went to learn all about the art of cupping and gain his foundational knowledge of coffee processing from Mr Jorge Villacorta (in Ernesto's opinion, one of the best cuppers in El Salvador).

During this time Ernesto was also building his own business. First he bought Finca Alaska, then Finca Los Andes, and then Finca La Ilusión; since then he has bought Finca Las Brumas.

So talented at cupping, Ernesto had the opportunity to participate in the national jury of the first Cup of Excellence in El Salvador. This led to a ten year love affair with the national jury of the Cup of Excellence.

"I met Steve in the ceremony of the El Salvador CoE 2008. I remember that he came to congratulate me for having won the first place in the CoE program, and the next day we went visit La Ilusión. I think that day was the beginning of this very special coffee relationship."

The Cup of Excellence is entwined in this story of how I came to meet Ernesto. I went to El Salvador on a buying trip in 2008, and I was visiting some of the farms that we buy from. I actually arrived the evening of the Cup of Excellence awards; after the ceremony I was walking around with a friend when I bumped into this guy who seemed very popular and introduced himself. He was Ernesto or, as I would come to know him, Neto. He'd just won the Cup of Excellence competition with his La Ilusión farm, the sister farm of Finca Alaska. Alaska is a farm we had bought from via the Cup of Excellence the year before.

Ernesto invited me to visit La Ilusión the next day. It was great to finally meet someone I had communicated with so many times via email.

Finca La Ilusión's coffee was used by the 2011 World Barista champion, Alejandro Mendez. That year I'd roasted the coffee, and it had been grown by Neto. There was a magical moment backstage in which I was stood, polishing glass, with Alejandro and Neto; the grower, roaster and barista stood together, preparing for the presentation. It's not too often you get such wonderful things happening, and it remains a special moment for me and for Ernesto.

The relationship has not been without its bumps. There were two years where we didn't buy from Ernesto, but bridges were built and we now buy everything from three of Ernesto's farms, and we are very close friends.

NAME: Ernesto Menendez

AGE: 41

IN COFFEE: 22 yrs

Your biggest influence in coffee: It's not a person; it's the the Cup of Excellence program.

Your proudest achievement in coffee: Really complicated to say ... my first place in the CoE El Salvador 2008, but maybe the first place of Alejandro Mendez in the WBC 2011 from La Ilusión and roasted by Has Bean. It was a really sublime moment in my life.

Favourite way to relax: Go to my farm and make a picnic with my family.

If you could grow coffee anywhere in the world apart from your own country, where and why: I'd love to grow coffee at the Yirgacheffe mountains, under wild forest. One of my dreams is to go to Ethiopia.

What's your favourite coffee time of the year: The harvesting season is the most special moment when you begin to see that all the effort of the year turns into a coffee cherry, which goes into a basket ready for the wet and dry process to finally put the passion into a coffee cup; the effort, work, dedication, and love and dreams of many people that are involved in the process.

EL SALVADOR

Finca San José

"Every time Stephen visits, even if we don't speak the same language, we communicate with signs and make weird faces and understand each other. I love his face when he is cupping the coffees and really likes something, and tries to tell me by signs that he looooooves it."

"My favourite varietal is Bourbon. It was my father's favourite varietal too. It's such a sweet cup, even if it's not a high-yielding varietal."

Gloria Rodriguez

I first met Gloria back in 2009, through her now-son-in-law and my good friend, Luis Rodriguez, and his now-wife Majo (Maria Jose). Luis and Majo were working for the Consejo (the government-run coffee association of El Salvador) and had become internet friends, and told me they had a farm I just had to see.

Gloria is a fourth generation coffee farmer. The story began in 1815, when José María Rodriguez and Josefina Rodriguez (great-grandparents) planted the first coffee trees with their own hands. Through the generations, the farm has passed through the hands of many committed farmers, like José's son Israel Rodriguez.

He was then followed by Jose Maria Rodriguez, who took care of the farm until it came to Gloria Mercedes Rodriguez Fontán, the most recent owner.

Ever the strong woman, Gloria has overcome gender barriers in an industry that has historically been the province of men, and personally supervises every step at the farm level.

> "Ever the strong woman, Gloria has overcome gender barriers in an industry that has historically been the province of men, and personally supervises every step at the farm level."

Gloria owns Finca Nejapa, Finca El Porvenir, Finca Nueva Granada, Finca San José (which she inherited from her father 22 years ago), and her own farm, which she has owned for 41 years, Finca Lagunita. There is also the recent addition from a couple of years ago of Finca Mamatita, which was an abandoned farm next door to San José that was just too good a deal to turn down.

The farms are all in the department of Ahuachapán near to the town of Apaneca, a vibrant town for coffee production.

With all these farms, Gloria needs a right-hand person to do all the day-to-day management, and one of Gloria's major blessings (her words, not mine) is to have Antonio Avelino as her farm manager or "mandador" (foreman). His level of commitment, knowledge and shared philosophy of quality makes him an integral part of this effort.

Some other work done to San José recently included three foliar fertilisations and two soil fertilisations, including one of organic fertiliser named "Ecomineral," which is based on soil studies to ensure specific requirements. Where possible, workers ply the farm with stem bending or "agobio," and they perform coffee shade pruning to balance sunlight and shade requirements under sustainable levels. They also perform weed control, mainly manually.

One of Gloria's commitments is to reinvest an important share of the economic benefits from this activity into the farms, impacting the people who toil the fields and maintaining the quality of the production chain from seed to cup.

She is a true role model farmer who isn't afraid of getting her hands dirty and making sure that the people who work for her share in her successes, of which there are many: she is a nine time Cup of Excellence award winner, and got first place in the El Salvador Coffee of the Year from the SCAA.

NAME: Gloria Rodriguez

AGE: 63

IN COFFEE: 41 yrs

Your biggest influence in coffee: This has to be my father, Jose María Rodriguez.

Your proudest achievement in coffee: Winning SCAA's Coffee of the Year award in 2011 with Finca San José. Also the first time I won CoE in 2007.

Biggest challenge facing you today: Climate change and leaf rust, and being able to cope with higher costs (in salaries, harvesting, and fertilisers).

Favourite way to relax: Going to the beach with friends and family, and spending lots of time with my grandson.

If you could grow coffee anywhere in the world apart from your own country, where and why: Maybe Nicaragua, because it's "safer" and there's less population density.

If you had a blank cheque, what would be the one investment you would make in the farm: I currently use an external mill to process our coffee. I would love to be able to build my own wet mill with my own people so I could have total control over the process.

EL SALVADOR

Finca La Gloria

"The biggest challenge facing me today is seeing so many of our neighbours going out of business. So many farms that are neglected close to ours means a lot of pressure with pest and plagues."

"From a small child my mum encouraged me to drink coffee. One of my earliest memories: that's what we do in El Salvador."

Luis Rodriguez

I love Luis – he is a geek like me. I first met Luis online on a coffee forum, while he was working as a coffee administrator for the Consejo (the national Salvadoran Coffee Council). At the time I had no idea he would go on to be a farmer, nor one of our most important contacts in El Salvador.

To my mind there was a golden age for El Salvadorian coffee, and this was around 2004–2010, when they seemed to get so many things right.

Around this time the Consejo was run by Ricardo Espitia, who really understood the emerging specialty coffee market. He was aided by two amazing people: Maria Jose Huezo (who is also in this book) and Luis Rodriguez himself (who has since married Maria Jose).

The reason everything was going so well was that the team was reaching out to the emerging barista community, being vocal on forums and being open to answering questions.

“One of the most memorable moments was to introduce Steve with Ernesto Menendez the year he won CoE. I knew Steve bought from his farm Alaska the year before and that he was around that year for the award ceremony, but overall being able to watch that relationship grow throughout the years has been great.”

It seems so obvious now, but at the time this was revolutionary and innovative.

So on my first trip to El Salvador I had to meet the man I'd spoken to for so long, and since then we have been good friends.

We share a passion for coffee varietals. We often share information as we find it, and when we get together it gets so geeky. I've learnt so much from our chats together.

Not only does he now have his own farm with Maria Jose, but he also helps with his mother-in-law's farms (Gloria Rodriguez, who is also in this book, is his mother-in-law), and he has been pivotal in helping Gloria and I be able to work together. But he was also vital in finding one of the most important varietals Gloria has found to date.

While walking around the farm checking for ripeness in a previous harvest time at Finca San José, Luis ended in front of a huge cluster of cherries which grabbed his attention. He arranged to get enough to sample them and see what might be in the cup. One of the most interesting facts was the amount of mucilage inside each cherry, which was twice as much as other varieties found at the farm.

At the moment, the varietal is still under scrutiny by geneticists. But the name “Elefante” was given to it temporarily by the family because of the bigger size of this bean compared to Bourbon, which is the more common variety at the farm.

In 2011, at the Specialty Coffee Association of America trade show and conference, a sample of Finca San José Elefante won El Salvador's Best of Origin at the Roaster's Guild Coffee of the Year event, and it also placed 4th overall in the same event, which had more than 120 submissions.

Luis is great friend who owns a farm, rather than a farmer who became a great friend. He is a unique man and a unique producer.

NAME: Luis Rodriguez

AGE: 39

IN COFFEE: 16 yrs

Your biggest influence in coffee: Ricardo Espitia (former boss at Salvadoran Coffee Council).

Your proudest achievement in coffee: Being part of the specialty coffee revolution in El Salvador a few years back, surrounded by so many interesting people from my country and worldwide.

Favourite way to relax: Having an ice cool beer or two.

If you could grow coffee anywhere in the world apart from your own country, where and why: Madagascar ... I would love to just go and plant all kinds of weird varieties and species there.

Favourite coffee varietal and why: A hard one, but perhaps Elefante because of how much I love the mucilage taste and its cup qualities, plus the story behind how we found it.

If you had a blank cheque, what would be the one investment you would make in the farm: I would love to create a coffee seed bank with as much of the germplasm available in the world using one half of the money, and I would plant my favourites with the rest.

Ethiopia

"Going to Yirgacheffe for the first time was a little like going on a pilgrimage: visiting the birthplace of coffee and then visiting the home of one of the most famous coffee regions is a must for a coffee roaster."

– Stephen Leighton

E T H I O P I A

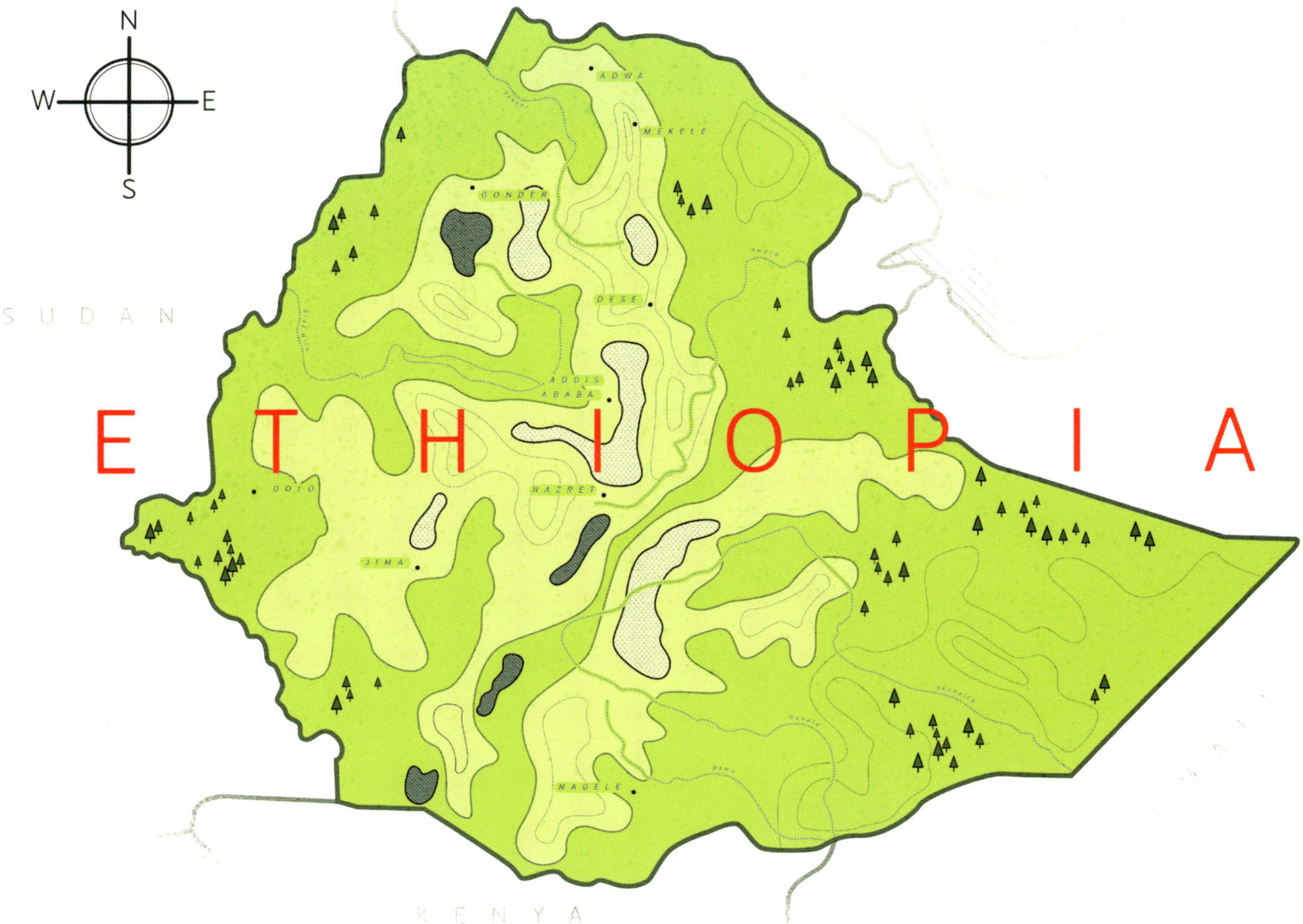

Ethiopia is often referred to as the "birthplace of coffee." Like every coffee story, this has to be taken with a pinch of salt, but there is no doubt it was the first place it was consumed and the place from which coffee was exported to the rest of the world; first to Yemen, then to Java, and then to the Americas and the rest of the coffee-producing world.

Coffee production in Ethiopia accounts for around 3% of the global coffee market and remains a very important part of the economy in Ethiopia. There are an estimated fifteen million people in Ethiopia relying on coffee production in some aspect for their livelihood. Coffee equates to around 35% of Ethiopia's total exports and around 60% of foreign income.

Ethiopia is surrounded in bureaucracy, rules and red tape, and is one of the last countries I have tried to export from. Even now I still use the services of an exporter to get coffee out of Ethiopia, even though I have a more relationship-based approach to buying.

Even with these barriers, Ethiopia has unique varietals with thousands of years of evolution and a remarkable set of processing and environmental conditions, all of which makes Ethiopian coffee some of the very best in the world.

Coffee Facts

Total production in 2016 (60 kg): 6,600,000
Percentage rise and fall on previous year: -1.7%
Internal consumption in 2016 (60 kg): 3,700,000
Consumption per capita: 2.26 kg per person per annum
Taste profile: Washed: Citrus, black tea and bergamot; sweet. **Natural:** blueberry, funky and fruity
Common varietals: Heirloom wild varietals
Coffee growing altitudes: 1,400 m.a.s.l. to 2,200 m.a.s.l.
Rank of coffee production: 5th in the world
Main buyers: United States, Germany and Japan
Unique problems: Government interference, bureaucratic processes, weather issues
Soil types: Rich with minerals, red, loamy soils

Country Facts

Population:
104,344,901 (2017)

Population density:
104 people per km²

Capital city:
Addis Ababa

Land mass:
999,541 km²

Currency:
Birr

ETHIOPIA

Mokanisa Bulega

"All my life, starting from the beginning until now, I am in coffee; also all my family's in the coffee business."

"I studied my primary school in Yirgalem and came to Addis Ababa to study my high school and college."

Israel Degefa Seme

Israel is one of the newest relationships I have in this book. For many years, Ethiopia has scared me as a place to do business because of the complexity and bureaucracy around coffee exports.

Added to this is the fact that most coffee in Ethiopia comes from cooperatives and not private farms. It all makes building long term, strong relationships difficult.

And even now, I am still using the services of an exporter to help me get this coffee out because of the red tape and special skills needed to source coffee from Ethiopia.

I first met Israel on the cupping table whilst in Ethiopia in 2016. I was presented with around 150 samples to cup through, and this one lot just shone out as one of exceptional quality. I love the descriptor parma violets, and this cup had a bagful of them.

Israel is a second generation coffee farmer who owns 20 wet mills across the different areas of southern Ethiopia, and 3 dry mills on top of that.

> “I was born on a coffee farm around Sidamo, Yirgalem, and grew up there. My parents are in the coffee farming business; my mum was selling her coffee in the bus station for the passengers.”

It was Ana Sora that made me brave enough to try to buy coffee from Ethiopia in a more relationship-based way.

This coffee farm covers 250 hectares, only 150 of which are currently producing; however, it is estimated that the remaining 100 hectares will be in full production by 2018. It has crazy altitude, ranging from 1,900 metres above sea level (m.a.s.l.) to 2,300 m.a.s.l. It is situated alongside the river Turo.

Currently the farm only produces natural coffee. However, in the future the river will be used as a water source to facilitate the processing of washed coffee. Israel plans to build a processing station on his land by 2018.

The farm itself is made up of forest land, through which there are many springs that feed into the river Turo. It is made up of green highland hills with steep slopes. The surrounding area is populated by smallholder farmers who are of Oromo ethnicity and speak Oromo. Israel believes that helping these farmers with education in husbandry and financial assistance is the only way to sustain coffee growing in Ethiopia.

Israel was born on a coffee farm near Sidamo, Yirgalem. Growing up there was where he found his love for coffee. His parents were both in the coffee industry but in different ways. His mum sold her coffee in the bus station for the passengers, whilst his father was a farmer.

As he got older, Israel studied at a primary school in Yirgalem, but to further his education he had to move to Addis Ababa to study at high school and college.

Nearby there is a secondary school called Yerba Buleye, which works with the farm to teach the children how to work and farm coffee. Israel also supports an orphanage in a neighbouring village.

I'm very pleased and proud to have found Israel and his coffee, and I hope that we are able to work together for many years to come.

NAME: Israel Degefa Seme

AGE: 30

IN COFFEE: 18 yrs

What's your favourite coffee time of the year: October–December, for the harvest and to see the farmers' smiley faces.

Favourite way to relax: By having a farmers' holiday and playing cultural music and dancing with them.

If you could grow coffee anywhere in the world apart from your own country, where and why: South Africa. I want to be a pioneer for coffee in the Cape Town and George areas. They have good farming technologies but not for coffee, and they have convenient areas for coffee plantations.

Favourite coffee you've had (not including yours): I haven't tried coffees from many different places. I like to drink west Arsi coffees.

Biggest challenge facing you today: The region's infrastructure is not good. For this reason we pay more to transport our coffee, and this makes production costs high. We also pay cash for cherries delivered to the wet mills, and we use a security house in the farm for all the money.

Guatemala

"Guatemala has such diversity in its Denominación de Origen program that it's like visiting eight countries in one, each one with a unique cup profile."

– Stephen Leighton

G U A T E M A L A

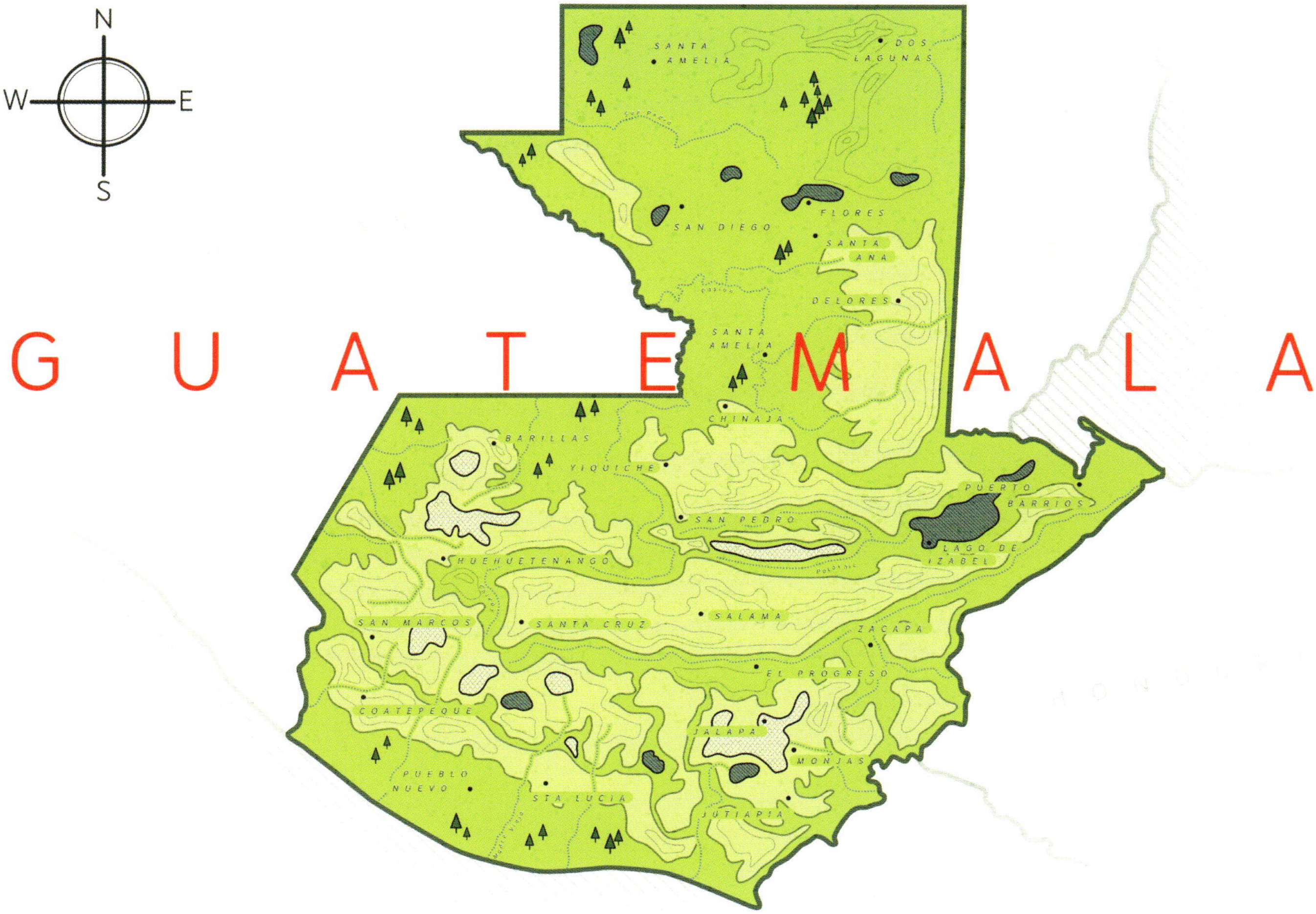

The coffee industry began in Guatemala in the 1850s and 1860s, initially with small plantations in the Amatitlán and Antigua areas in the southwest. Development was slow because much of the production was from smallholder growers with a lack of resources.

The influx of foreign investment in the late 19th century saw an explosion of progress that, up until recent years, made Guatemala the biggest coffee producer in Central America.

Guatemalan coffee production peaked at the turn of the 21st century, when it reached around 8,400,000 bags. Since 2004, however, there has been a dramatic decline in yields.

Anacafé (Asociación Nacional del Café) was established in 1960 as a national coffee association, representing all coffee producers in Guatemala. It is funded by a 1% levy on every coffee transaction. Anacafé has focused on specialty coffee to raise prices.

Separating the growing regions into different taste profiles has been a marketing success, making Guatemala one of the leading lights in specialty coffee.

Coffee Facts

Total production in 2016 (60 kg): 3,500,000
Percentage rise and fall on previous year: +2.3%
Internal consumption in 2016 (60 kg): 340,000
Consumption per capita: 1.27 kg per person per annum
Taste profile: Diverse, fruity, complex, acidic and sweet cups
Common varietals: Bourbon, Caturra and Catuai
Coffee growing altitudes: 1,300 m.a.s.l. to 2,000 m.a.s.l.
Rank of coffee production: 10th in the world
Main buyers: USA, Japan and Canada
Unique problems: Urban expansion, city gang issues, labour problems
Soil types: Volcanic red loam

Country Facts

Population:
17,005,497 (2017)

Population density:
159 people per km²

Capital city:
Guatemala City

Land mass:
107,153 km²

Currency:
Quetzal

GUATEMALA

Finca Baquelito

> "My biggest influences come from my previous generations of family, because we are fifth generation coffee farmers. Everything I have learned about coffee is from them."

"I love the variety Catuai because of its ability to express fruit characteristics in the cup."

Juan Carlos Estevez

Juan Carlos is one of the quieter producers we buy from. No noise, no fuss; just amazing coffee. One of the many reasons I wanted to produce this book was so Juan Carlos – and people like him – became the coffee superstar he so deserves to be, and so you get to understand why his coffee is so good.

Grown in one of Guatemala's most challenging coffee regions, the farm is located in Alta Verapaz, also known as Cobán.

The farm, Finca Baquelito, is almost hidden in the mountains and the coffee trees are flooded with rainforest.

It is located between 1,000 and 1,450 metres above sea level and covers a huge 158 hectares of growing area. Cobán is challenging because it has two main growing seasons: the rainy season and the rainier season. The constantly high humidity and constant rain make it a difficult place to cultivate coffee in traditional ways.

“As a fifth generation coffee farmer, I am blessed with all the experience around me.”

But the clouds and cooler temperatures mean that the coffee cherry maturation takes a little longer than normal, and that allows the flavour characteristics to really develop.

This is what gives Baquelito its unique cup profile. The Estevez family took over the farm in 1976, although they are fifth generation coffee producers. Juan Carlos became more involved in the 1990s. During Juan Carlos' time on the farm, it has undergone a huge replanting of new varieties of coffee to work with the challenging conditions – varieties such as Catimor 5175 and Catuai, imported from Costa Rica. Another major phase of replanting happened in 2013–2014: new varieties came, such as Castillo, Pacamara and Lempira, all fed from the family's own nursery on the farm where they produce plants from their guaranteed seed stock.

The coffee harvest season starts in October and ends in March. But Baquelito doesn't just produce coffee; it has other crops, such as cardamom, pine forestry and fruits, and it has several natural water sources that nourish the area.

Added to this, the geography of the farm is unique. It is located in a basin where there is the permanent presence of two thermal sources: the cold coming from the northeast and the hot from the southwest, which converge to produce a special microclimate.

When I first met Juan Carlos, I asked him what makes his coffee special. He replied: “The way it is cultivated, the location of the farm with its microclimate and the effort of all those who work on the farm to produce a good coffee.” He is always quick to praise the team he has working with him, whereas many farmers are keen to praise themselves. Again, another side of the man who is incredibly humble.

Not happy with just producing great coffee, Juan Carlos wants to make it even better. He has plans for the future for more varietal experiments, and has invested to protect the local forest areas on the farm, preserving areas from farming and leaving the natural habitat.

NAME: Juan Carlos Estevez

AGE: 49

IN COFFEE: 25 yrs

Favourite coffee you've had (not including yours): I like the variety "Marago" that we produce in Guatemala. Its cup profile is for its characteristics: it's just chocolate in a cup.

Biggest challenge facing you today: Today we face huge problems with global warming, which is affecting every part of coffee farming. We also suffer with a high cost of production in Guatemala, which makes it hard to produce speciality coffee.

Favourite way to relax: Enjoying the unique landscapes within my farm and being at one with the nature.

If you could grow coffee anywhere in the world apart from your own country, where and why: I would not change my country, because Guatemala is unique in its climate and its richness of soil.

What's your favourite coffee time of the year: I love all times of the coffee cycle. Each of them is special and unique, but there is something magical about the flowering cycle.

GUATEMALA

Finca Ciudad Vieja Los Jocotales

"My biggest accomplishment is to have a plate of food every day, since I spent days without being able to eat as a child. And that makes me proud that my family has safe food."

"One of my proudest achievements is to be one of the first producers in Guatemala to be working in the honey process."

Jairo Alexander Illescas Perez

Alex is one of the youngest producers I work with, but also one of the most dynamic. I first met him in January 2013 in a back street of Ciudad Vieja. It's a small town just outside of Antigua, the famous and ancient city in Guatemala. I met Alex whizzing about on a motorbike when Raul Rodas, World Barista Champion and my friend, took me to meet him.

Being a fourth generation coffee producer, Alex has spent his whole life surrounded by coffee. Growing up, he was also surrounded by women. He had five siblings, all sisters. His father died when he was eight, and he was the second youngest, meaning he was very much a baby of the family.

Growing up, there were happy and tough times. Alex recalls instances where times were hard and even the basics of food could be in short supply.

He told me there were times when the family would not be able to eat, and he is driven to be able to support his family. Talking to me for this book, he said that his proudest achievement was

“Alex had an idea that he wanted to do the honey process for the coffee. Honeying is very common in Central America, but not so in Guatemala.”

that his family had a plate of food on the table every day and that they were safe.

That first visit was crazy to say the least. He took me to the family farm, which had been his grandfather's farm. He told me that his grandfather had allowed him to have a small amount of the coffee to market it. I had the feeling that Alex had been badgering him for months (if not years) about this, and it was a final step to get rid of him.

Alex had an idea that he wanted to honey process the coffee. Honeying is very common in Central America, but not so in Guatemala.

But Alex knew that he could process small amounts of the coffee himself this way, taking away the need to wash the coffee and not have to use natural process for the coffee. It also gave him a unique marketing strategy to be one of the first honey processors in Guatemala.

Pulping the coffee himself, he took the coffee to his uncle's house (and I mean house) and used his roof space, where normally they would relax and watch the sun go down in the evenings, to dry the coffee.

I remember that visit to the roof, the first time in Ciudad Vieja, and thinking "what the heck is going on here?" But I was interested enough to try the coffee, and ever since then I have fallen in love with the coffee farm, and Alex's drive and passion.

The following year when I visited, Alex had used the money he had got for the coffee to set up a temporary mill for that year so he could also wash and naturally process the family's coffee, too.

Not everything goes to plan, and the following year the mill was sold to a developer for housing. But using his determination, he is renting space at a local mill to still have ultimate control of the processing.

He has now set up a coffee shop in the town's back streets and is a real entrepreneur in the world of coffee.

NAME: Jairo Alexander Illescas Perez

AGE: 29

IN COFFEE: 10 yrs

Your biggest influence in coffee: No money has exchanged hands for this, but it's Stephen Leighton. He was one of my first buyers, and someone who believed in the work I was doing.

If you had a blank cheque, what would be the one investment you would make in the farm: I would love to build a wet and dry mill to process the whole family's farms.

What makes your coffee special: I think it's because I am in love with the tradition of farming in Guatemala, but I can also see that I can add to this tradition by looking at the larger coffee world and learning from other producers.

Favourite way to relax: I love to walk around the farm on my own amongst the coffee trees, taking in the sights and sounds.

If you could grow coffee anywhere in the world apart from your own country, where and why: I love Guatemala, but if it was anywhere then I'd love to grow coffee in the birthplace of coffee: Ethiopia.

GUATEMALA

Finca La Soledad

"Coffee has taught me a lot of things, but the most important is probably to be patient. I'm a person who likes to see results fast, and see coffee develop on the production side of the chain."

"The one thing that is changing now is weather patterns. The last four years have been hard for us without steady weather conditions."

Raul Pérez

Raul has grown up around coffee. He comes from a fifth generation coffee farming family on his father's side, and a third generation family on his mother's side. Coffee has always been part of his life. He has told me about stories his grandparents would share with him about their experiences.

But I think it's fair to say that Raul has made plenty of his own coffee stories in his ten years of involvement in the speciality coffee industry.

It was ten years ago when Raul first became involved in the family business. After living in Guatemala City in his youth (so he was able to go to a good school and university), he returned to the farm where his family had still been working and commuting.

This coincided with a visit from an international buyer who made the family view coffee production in a different way. The speciality market was blossoming and the visitor gave them new ideas for varietals, picking, and processing that changed the direction of their farm and their cup quality.

As Raul puts it, they began to work in a "more interactive way."

Finca La Soledad has been a Pérez family coffee farm since 1895. The farm is located in Acatenango, near to the Acatenango volcano. It has a great microclimate and an altitude of 1,650 metres above sea level.

The Pérez family invested heavily in their mill, rebuilding it with the environment in mind. They have a clever system through which they are able to recycle the water they use for processing many times.

"We want to reach the specialty market on the coffee it demands. It requires more dedication and attention to small details, and we believe it makes the difference at the end."

Raul and his dad Henio work together on the farm to raise quality standards every day. Since that visit which sparked the changes, they have built a cupping and roasting lab on the farm and Raul has been roasting and cupping samples of days' pickings so they can learn at farm level what they can do to improve the cup.

The first time I met Raul was at a friend's wedding in Guatemala. I didn't know him (like most of the other guests), but we got talking and I enjoyed his company. At no time did he try to push his coffee on me, and I think only in passing did he say his family worked in coffee.

Raul was so kind he offered to take us back to our hotel that evening to save us having to get in a dodgy cab in Guatemala City.

I have an exporting partner in Guatemala who sent me this amazing sample, which I decided there and then we had to buy. It was only after I had committed to buying the coffee that I found out it was from Raul's farm.

Since then I've been lucky enough to visit the farm and meet the whole family. A fond memory that will stay with me is sitting on the unused drying patio with them all, enjoying a beer and watching the sun go down. They are a professional team and a lovely, warm family.

NAME: Raul Pérez

AGE: 35

IN COFFEE: 10 yrs

Biggest challenge facing you today: Many. Roya and low productivity have played a big role in our challenges in the last six years, but just recently the low amount of rain has been a big issue for producing and processing our coffees.

Favourite coffee you've had (not including yours): I had the chance to drink many coffees, but Ethiopian and Kenyan coffees are amazing in flavours and complexity – way different from Central America.

What's your favourite coffee time of the year: Harvest, for sure. It is the culmination of a year's worth of hard work and struggles.

If you had a blank cheque, what would be the one investment you would make in the farm: I would invest in three things. One will be improving housing for our workers. It is good but we want to make it better for them and keep them happy to work. Secondly, I would invest in having more beds to dry the coffee. Thirdly, I would create more water reservoirs for people and for processing the coffee.

GUATEMALA

Finca El Limon

"One of the funniest moments when Stephen visits is watching him eat Kaqlk or 'Chunto soup.' He puts so much chilli in it that he starts to sweat, turns red and gets the snot."

"My coffee is special because of the effort and dedication of my family that is translated to a culture of work, to which a well-defined vision is added; and to which all days and all mornings we put the passion needed. But above all, the blessing of God."

Guadalupe Alberto Reyes Aguilar

Alberto (Beto from now on) is one of my favourite people to visit every year. His family are the most welcoming and lovely people, and I always get way over-fed with delicious traditional food. But most of all, the farm (El Limon) is a picture book farm that was hidden away from the world of specialty coffee.

Let me take you back to 2013. Has Bean was well established in El Salvador, Costa Rica and Nicaragua, but strangely I'd never ventured into Guatemala. I'm not sure why, but it was somewhere we had missed.

A drunken conversation with the world barista champion of the time (from Guatemala) in a bar in Moscow, Russia, led to an invite to come meet some of his coffee producing friends.

I don't think Raul Rodas expected me to take him up on his kind offer, but I'm ever the rude man; I turned up at his house and crashed for a week while he introduced me to lots of his coffee people.

“I have two favourite times of the year. One is initially the winter, because it’s the time of the sowing. The second one is the flowering time, which is when the coffee responds to our efforts, and it is what motivates us to continue working.”

We did the normal trips to Antigua, Amatitlán and Huehuetenango, where everyone else treads. I thought we were done, but Raul had one more trick up his sleeve – he took me to a region to which few venture.

He took me to Beto’s farm, El Limon, located around an hour’s drive to the east of Guatemala City in the small town of Palencia. This farm sits at an altitude of between 1,600 and 1,800 metres above sea level.

Palencia is not part of the eight regions of coffee as defined by Anacafé, but you can see a lot of development in the zone, and this farm is a perfect example of that development. I like being in places that are working to be hot and up-and-coming, as well as those that are established players.

One of the main reason I love El Limon is the desire to experiment. The farm mostly produces Bourbon and Caturra, but Beto also plays around with other varietals. The experimentation comes from Beto’s motivation; he has really focused on the farm. He wanted to take more care in every step they take – from picking to processing, to shipping – and also take more care in the agronomy of the farm.

This is very much a family affair: his wife and son also work on the farm, along with Beto’s siblings. In fact, his son (Beto Junior) is studying agronomy at the local college for the benefit of the farm.

The whole family is involved – sons, daughters, brother, cousins – and everyone takes part in the running of the farm.

Beto is enjoying his second term as Mayor of Palencia, which is a very involved role that brings him into regular contact with the president and other political figures in Guatemala. In the community, Beto knows everyone and everyone knows him.

I’m so happy to have found Beto and his family, and even more happy we get to share his coffee with the world.

NAME: Guadalupe Alberto Reyes Aguilar

AGE: 52

IN COFFEE: 19 yrs

Your proudest achievement in coffee: To have started like a person who walked barefoot in the streets of Palencia, being a son of peasants, and today be positioned with my family working among the best coffees in the world.

Biggest challenge facing you today: Without a doubt it's the climate change, to which is added the very competitive market's demand, along with a fall of coffee prices. However, we trust that with quality we will come out ahead and that our customers will continue buying our coffee for its flavour and its quality.

Espresso or Filter: Espresso.

Favourite coffee varietal and why: Pacamara is the first variety with which we work on the farm, and currently we have worked hard to have a larger extent of Pacamara. We bet on Pacamara, and while we are alive we will have Pacamara in our farm.

If you could grow coffee anywhere in the world apart from your own country, where and why: I would go to Colombia with eyes closed. Such great coffee.

Honduras

“As the biggest producer of coffee in Central America, there is no doubt there are some amazing Honduran coffees out there. But it’s somewhere I’ve found I have to look a little harder to find that special quality.”

– Stephen Leighton

Coffee is thought to have been introduced to Honduras by visiting traders in the late 18th century.

Records show coffee was being grown in the late 19th century, but on a very small scale. Numerous governments failed to excite Hondurans about growing coffee – they chose to grow the lucrative banana instead.

Widespread coffee cultivation did not begin until the second half of the 20th century. While the banana industry is owned by a few big players, coffee has become the entrepreneur's choice: over 90% of the roughly 120,000 coffee farmers are classed as small producers.

Honduras punches above its weight when it comes to coffee. In 2011 it became Central America's biggest coffee producer. It's ranked sixth in the world, even though it's a tiny nation.

It has problems: premature ageing, cross-border coffee smuggling, and issues with shipping lines at harvest mean not all Honduran coffee arrives in consuming countries in as good a condition as it was. But at last we are beginning to see real quality from this amazing country.

Coffee Facts

Total production in 2016 (60 kg): 5,800,000

Percentage rise and fall on previous year: +2.9%

Internal consumption in 2016 (60 kg): 345,000

Consumption per capita: 2.6 kg per person per annum

Taste profile: Juicy acidity, zingy and complex

Common varietals: Caturra, Typica and Bourbon

Coffee growing altitudes: 700 m.a.s.l. to 2,000 m.a.s.l.

Rank of coffee production: 6th in the world

Main buyers: Japan and Europe

Unique problems: High crime and violence, and lack of port space at busy times of harvest

Soil types: Volcanic origin / wooded

Country Facts

Population:
8,304,677 (2017)

Population density:
74 people per km²

Capital city:
Tegucigalpa

Land mass:
111,878 km²

Currency:
Lempira

HONDURAS

Finca Cerro Azul

"I enjoy a filter coffee because it allows me to enjoy its subtle notes better. I may be predisposed to filter simply by growing up without access to an espresso machine, but I feel an espresso robs drinkers of the elegant sweetness, acidity and flavours that evolve."

"Stephen and my family formed an instant friendship from the first time we met. It seemed only fate we should begin working together."

Erwin Mierisch

I could write a whole book about this man, and somebody should. Originating from Nicaragua, exiled and educated in Texas because of the troubles with the Sandinista government in the late '80s in Nicaragua, and now owning his own farm in Honduras ... if it's there to be done, Erwin has done it. Erwin was the first ever person I met at origin, and is someone I class as a true friend.

Although he's a fourth generation coffee grower, it's not been without its troubles. Erwin did not start his career in coffee. In the 1980s, the Sandinista government confiscated the family coffee farms, forcing the entire family into exile in the USA. Facing the stark reality of a future without the family farms, he entered college seeking studies and knew he would need to excel within the business world of the USA. He graduated after sucessfully studying petroleum engineering.

The winds of fate changed and his family regained the family farms from the Nicaraguan government in 1991/1992.

“Processing coffee is my favourite part of the year. In the field, it takes a full year to yield results. Within 3 months of processing any experiment, development and evaluation can produce results in as little as 15 to 30 days. These 90 days are often frantic, and sometimes frustrating and rewarding.”

In 1994 he realised how little he knew about coffee, so set about immersing himself in it. He focused firstly on the technical side of running a farm, but then also on the educational side by organising the Cup of Excellence in Nicaragua in 2005. He went on to become a head judge for many Cup of Excellences all over the world. This was where I first met him, when he looked after all the international judges on my first trip outside of Europe, and we solidified our new friendship.

Erwin and I have many stories together, but I had forgotten about this one until he recalled it. “Stephen was accompanying a buying group. The group was dispersed amongst several trucks, one of which I was driving. Stephen led the expedition on an ATV with another roaster riding with him. Stephen left us in the dust, literally. After several minutes and quite a few curves in the path, we pull up to find Stephen kneeling next to the prone figure of the roaster on the ground. Stephen was frantic, waving at us to hurry up. I darted from our truck to aid the hurt roaster. A million things flashed through my mind: how were we to get emergency services to such a remote location; notification of the incident to his family; liability; and a world of other anxieties. Just as we approached and real panic was about to set in, they both screamed ‘got you!’ And burst out laughing. Ten years later, I guess I can laugh at it too. “

In 2011 Erwin started the project of revitalising Finca Cerro Azul in the region of the national park, Azul Meámbar. It’s in Siguatepeque, Comayagua, Honduras, and is across from Finca El Cielito, Santa Barbára. The farm lies on the other side of Lake Yojoa, and is blessed with microclimates and conditions that are familiar to the family because they are similar to the ones they experience on their lands in Nicaragua.

It’s the only Honduran coffee I’ve bought for the last few years, and that’s because you can taste all of Erwin’s experience and knowledge in every cup.

NAME: Erwin Mierisch

AGE: 51

IN COFFEE: 23 yrs

Your biggest influence in coffee: My mother, Maria Ligia McEwan, has been the biggest influence in the area of farming. She taught me not only efficiency on a personal and business level, but also the very fundamentals to treat all people with respect and fairness.

Your proudest achievement in coffee: I'm especially proud of our efforts in mentoring and training other producers in Honduras, El Salvador and Mexico to their own CoE wins.

Favourite coffee varietal and why: Yellow Pacamara. This new varietal, with great potential owing to its diverse flavour profile, has pronounced pineapple, passion fruit, black pepper, honey and stone fruit overtones.

Favourite way to relax: Horseback riding and fishing. Yet finding time to enjoy these things proves to be difficult. The best times for fishing conflict with chores on the farm. Furthermore, using horses for the workings on the farm is time consuming and antiquated by the advent of ATVs.

If you could grow coffee anywhere in the world apart from your own country, where and why: Growing and producing coffee is synonymous with family, so Nicaragua will always be my choice, because my family and heart reside there. If indulged and allowed to relocate my family with me, I'd be tempted to try the original birthplace of coffee: Ethiopia.

India

"India is often disregarded by coffee professionals because of its lack of acidity and high Robusta production. But because of its low acidity and familiar coffee-like flavours, it's the perfect gateway coffee for new consumers into the world of coffee."

– Stephen Leighton

INDIA

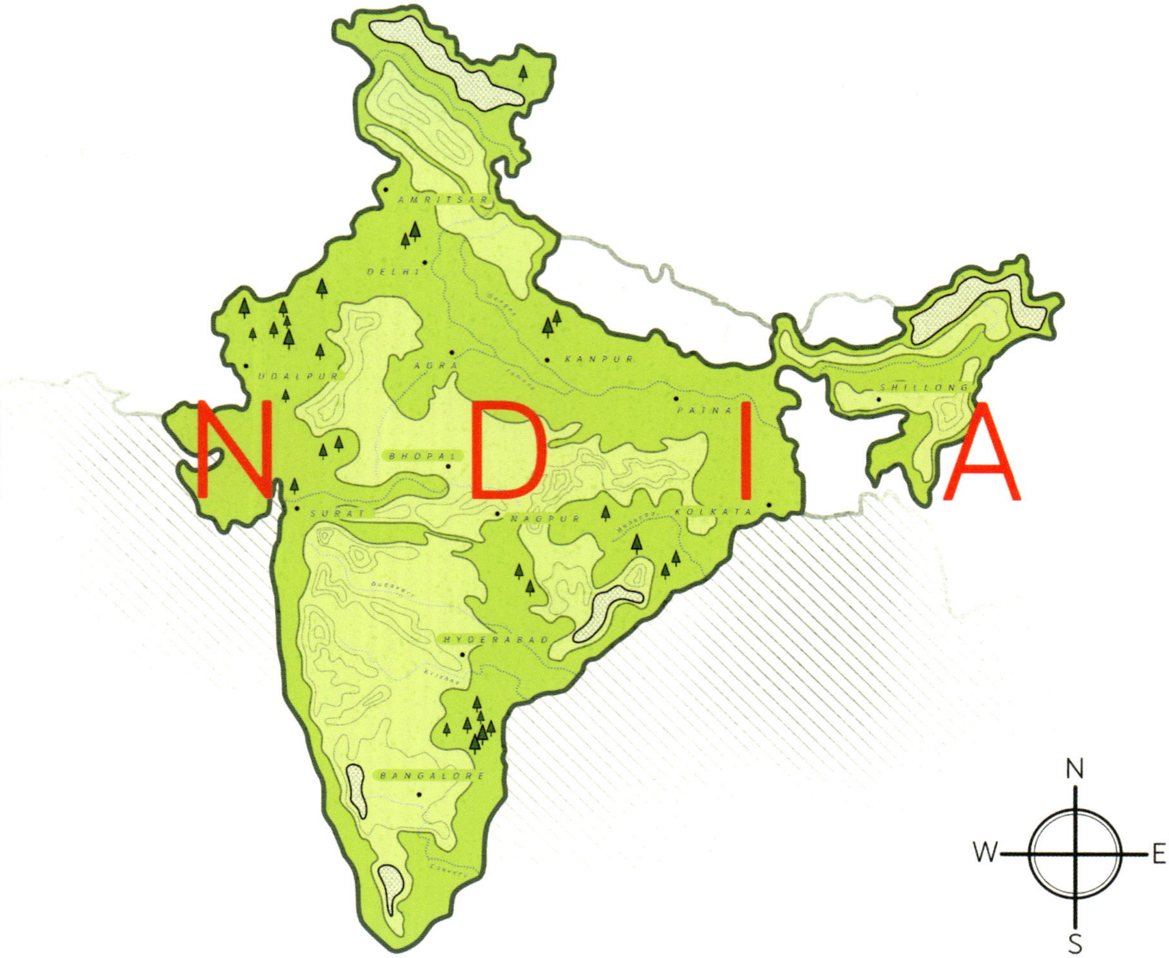

It is believed that coffee was introduced into India in the 1600s, accomplished upon the planting of "Seven seeds" of "Mocha" by the holy saint Baba Budan in his garden.

But it was not until the 18th century that the commercial plantations of coffee began, after intervention from the colonial British. However, this was short-lived; a decline in production in the 1870s due to leaf rust saw many of the farms turn into tea plantations.

The Coffee Board of India was formed in 1942. This saw an upturn in production and demand. Much of this demand was due to the growing internal market. Although consumption per annum is around 0.09 kg per person, when you have a population of 1,342,512,706 that equates to 1.9 million 60 kg bags per year.

Because of the low lands and the climate, India is well suited to growing Robusta. Only around 30% of production is Arabica.

"Monsooning" is a process unique to India. This is where the natural coffee is exposed to the monsoon rain for three to four months, causing the beans to swell and lose the original acidity, and resulting in a unique flavour profile. The coffee is unique to the Malabar Coast of Karnataka and Kerala.

Coffee Facts

Total production in 2016 (60 kg): 5,333,000
Percentage rise and fall on previous year: -8.1%
Internal consumption in 2016 (60 kg): 1,900,000
Consumption per capita: 0.09 kg per person per annum
Taste profile: Heavy, big body, low acidity
Common varietals: Kent, Cauvery, Tafarikela and San Ramon
Coffee growing altitudes: 800 m.a.s.l. to 1,600 m.a.s.l.
Rank of coffee production: 7th in the world
Main buyers: Russia, USA and Germany
Unique problems: Growing economy, increasing internal coffee demand
Soil types: Rich alluvial

Country Facts

Population:
1,342,512,706 (2017)

Population density:
452 people per km²

Capital city:
New Delhi

Land mass:
2,972,892 km²

Currency:
Rupee

INDIA

Bibi Plantation

"I learnt how to run the coffee farm by interacting with friends and learning along the way. Every day and month there was something new to learn."

"Twenty-seven years later,
I think I'm starting to enjoy
the farm quite a bit."

Faiz Moosakutty

Indian coffee is not seen as "cool" in the speciality coffee scene. You rarely see a barista at a competition waxing lyrical about this new Indian coffee they have found (in fact, you never do). India is often disregarded by coffee professionals because of its lack of acidity and high Robusta production.

But because of its low acidity, familiar coffee-like flavour and big body, it's the perfect gateway coffee for new consumers into the world of coffee. I know this because Faiz Moosakutty's Indian Bibi plantation Peaberry was one of my forays into speciality coffee. It has huge body, tobacco-like aftertaste and amazing coffee-like taste.

Faiz was a reluctant coffee farmer and, in fact, may have been bribed to take over the farm. He recalled the story of how he became a coffee producer to me.

"I returned from America in 1990 after completing university. I knew nothing about coffee, although my father had been looking after Bibi Plantation (our coffee farm) since the early 1960s. My father passed away in 1983.

“Due to ever-increasing climate changes and the ever-increasing temperatures year by year, we have stuck with growing fine quality washed Arabica coffee. Farms around us have all changed to growing Robusta.”

So my mother let me go to university in America on one condition: that I return and look after the coffee farm. I agreed and here I am, 27 years later, enjoying it quite a bit.

It has been a challenge to learn. It is also unique in that every year it is different because of various factors, but I would say mainly because of weather patterns and the ever-changing aspect of nature.

I learnt how to run the coffee farm by interacting with friends and learning along the way. Every day and month there was something new to learn, but eventually after I would say two years, our farm kind of settled into a set schedule of operations; to be honest, we have followed it ever since.”

The farm is five hours’ drive towards the coast from Bangalore. It’s near the small town of Suntikoppa (population: 20,000) among the Coorg hills of southern India. This is the heart of the coffee growing area in Karnataka, and all around lie small-to-medium sized farms.

While the farm is not officially certified organic, no chemical weed killers are used. Weeds are removed by hand so that the cut plants form a natural green compost.

We have worked with Faiz for thirteen years now, and every year I get so excited when the pre-shipment samples arrive. It’s like going back in time to that first cupping where I fell for the coffee. I’m guilty of not taking this coffee home every weekend, but when it lands it’s something I crave: what I like to call a “drinking” coffee.

I’ve not yet been able to visit Faiz, but he did come to visit me one time at the roastery in Stafford, and was confused by our craziness. He is a very kind and gentle person with an amazing feel around him. I was a little fanboy-like.

I don’t care if Indian coffee is not cool; I only care if it’s tasty, and Faiz manages to produce not only one of the best coffees from India, but one of the best coffees in the world.

NAME: Faiz Moosakutty

AGE: 51

IN COFFEE: 27 yrs

Your proudest achievement in coffee: Setting up one of the first private sector dry mills in the coffee industry here in our area.

Biggest challenge facing you today: The ever-increasing weather temperatures and the lack of rainfall in the sub-continent of India. It is posing a huge challenge to growing coffee.

Favourite way to relax: Watching TV and listening to music – and I like a good cup of coffee!

Favourite coffee varietal and why: Arabica SL 795: a very high quality Arabica coffee that was being grown in India for its yield and the productivity of coffee. Unfortunately, over the years it has been phased out in India due to the menace of pests – the coffee stem borer.

If you had a blank cheque, what would be the one investment you would make in the farm: To have a solution to the pest problem: to get rid of the white stem borer that is destroying the Arabica coffee industry in India.

Kenya

"As a coffee professional, you always remember the time you tasted your first "Great" Kenyan. I can still taste it today."

– Stephen Leighton

KENYA

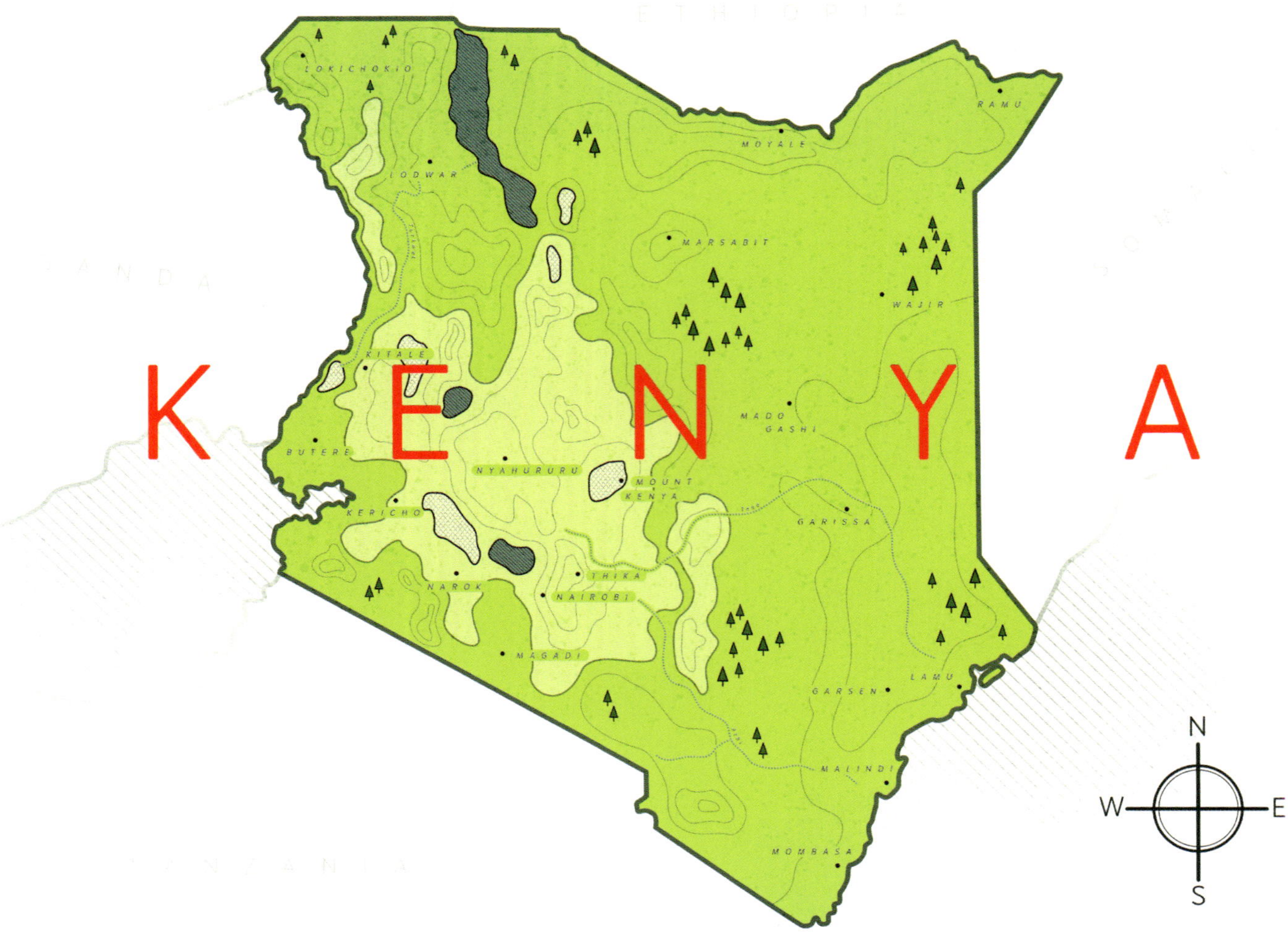

Although a neighbour of Ethiopia (the birthplace of coffee), Kenya was late to the party in the world of coffee. It is believed to have been introduced to Kenya in 1893 by the Holy Ghost Fathers (a Roman Catholic congregation of priests) using trees from Réunion Island. However, it was not until the 1900s that Kenya saw an explosion in coffee production, with the British planting on a much larger scale during their colonisation.

Dominated by cooperatives, around 70% of the country's coffee is produced by smallholder farmers who deliver their cherry to cooperative washing stations. The other 30% is made of estate farms owned by individuals, although this is on the decline; demand for land means that developments are more profitable than growing coffee.

1934 saw the birth of the Kenyan coffee auction in Nairobi, which is seen as a transparent distribution system that has maintained high prices for the country's coffee.

Much of the plant stock comes from the SL 28 and SL 34 varietals that were developed by Scott Labs in 1931. Originally developed for their resistance to drought, they have since become prized for their unique cup profile of blackcurrants and high acidity.

Coffee Facts

Total production in 2016 (60 kg): 783,000

Percentage rise and fall on previous year: -.07%

Internal consumption in 2016 (60 kg): 50,000

Consumption per capita: 0.07 kg per person per annum

Taste profile: Bright, high acidity, blackcurrant, winey

Common varietals: SL 28, SL34, Ruiru 11, Batian, K7

Coffee growing altitudes: 1,200 m.a.s.l. to 2,300 m.a.s.l.

Rank of coffee production: 16th in the world

Main buyers: Germany, USA, United Kingdom and Sweden

Unique problems: Drought, disease and urbanisation of the countryside

Soil types: Volcanic red

Country Facts

Population:
48,466,928 (2017)

Population density:
85 people per km²

Capital city:
Nairobi

Land mass:
569,295 km²

Currency:
Shilling

KENYA

Kiriga Estate

"My favourite time of the coffee year is after I have personally made the last coffee delivery to the dry mill, as it marks the end of yet another season successfully completed."

"I am a third generation coffee farmer. My grandfather, whom I am named after, planted our first coffee bushes in the 1950s."

Dr Brian Gakunga

Brian has been involved in coffee farming for 41 years, but he took over from his late father 10 years ago as full manager and proud co-owner of Kiriga Coffee Estate.

Since then Brian has strived to make his farm one of the leading coffee estates in Kenya, producing some of the most unique and amazing coffee available.Brian's late father encouraged his children to pursue their own careers, and so Brian studied to become a veterinary doctor and then proceeded into pharmaceutical sales. He attained senior management positions in two regional multinational organisations: Fresenius Kabi (German – Regional Manager, East Africa) and Novartis Pharma (Swiss – Sales Manager, East and Central Africa). During this period, he also studied for a Masters in Business Administration in Strategic Management.

This international experience was instrumental when he took over the running of the farm. Brian was not impressed by the status quo in the coffee farming sector and began to try to understand why coffee farmers were not getting the returns they so desperately deserved.

"During my first meeting with Steve, after going around the farm, he looked around and identified a spot on the grass in the house compound. He proceeded to make himself comfortable and started filming himself. He was completely oblivious of anything or anyone around him. It was the weirdest thing."

He could see that many of the surrounding estates were abandoning coffee farming and selling their land for property development, turning their backs on coffee growing.

He enrolled in a farm and factory management course at the Coffee Research Foundation to understand coffee farming better from a professional point of view.

After his course, he embarked on changing the way he processed coffee at his wet mill, and immediately noticed a remarkable improvement in his cup.

Seen as the face of the "youth" at 37 years old, he was introduced by government and other stakeholders in local and international forums as the face of the future coffee farmer. At the time, the average age of a coffee farmer was 60 to 65 years old. Since then there has been a big upturn in younger people getting involved in coffee farming, which is something Brian is rightly proud of.

His efforts were appreciated by the government and the rest of the coffee industry, and Brian was to become the first Chairman of the Nairobi Coffee Exchange (NCE). A transitional exchange committee was implemented, and his mandate was to improve systems and show a positive change. His proudest moment was when he made Kenyan auction history and wrote out cheques to farmers worth millions of shillings for their coffee samples delivered to the NCE; something that never happened before his tenure.

The way I found Brian is an interesting story, because he kind of found me. I bought his coffee back in 2011 from an importer. I always had a problem building something long term in Kenya because of the auction system.

But Brian reached out to me after finding an archived review I had written, in which I was waxing lyrical about his coffee. So Brian (and his American friend Jim) started a war of attrition on email, encouraging me to come visit. I caved, and the rest, as they say, is history.

NAME: Dr Brian Gakunga

AGE: 47

IN COFFEE: 41 yrs

Biggest challenge facing you today: Global warming. The farms are warmer and the rivers are drier. It's not raining as much, making irrigation a challenge.

Favourite way to relax: At any of our game parks watching the wild animals from the safety of my car as I enjoy my favourite Guinness Kubwa Baridi.

If you had a blank cheque, what would be the one investment you would make: There's a few. I'd drill a bore hole to get a constant supply of clean drinking water for the workers and irrigation for the coffee plants. I'd also buy 20 cows to provide another source of income to take care of some of the costs of running the estate, and to provide milk as a nutritional source for the children of the Kiriga family.

What makes your coffee special: Good farming practices, and a generous serving of TLC – Tender Loving Care – from the entire Kiriga family, our workers.

Favourite coffee varietal and why: A Batian and SL 28 blend with a little Ruiru 11 gives an amazing cup.

KENYA

Kieni Factory

"My favourite coffee varietal is Batian, because it produces more per tree and is less demanding on inputs – especially chemicals – because it is less affected by many diseases."

"I am a family man. My family is young, but they enjoy assisting with the harvesting as they enjoy the exercise."

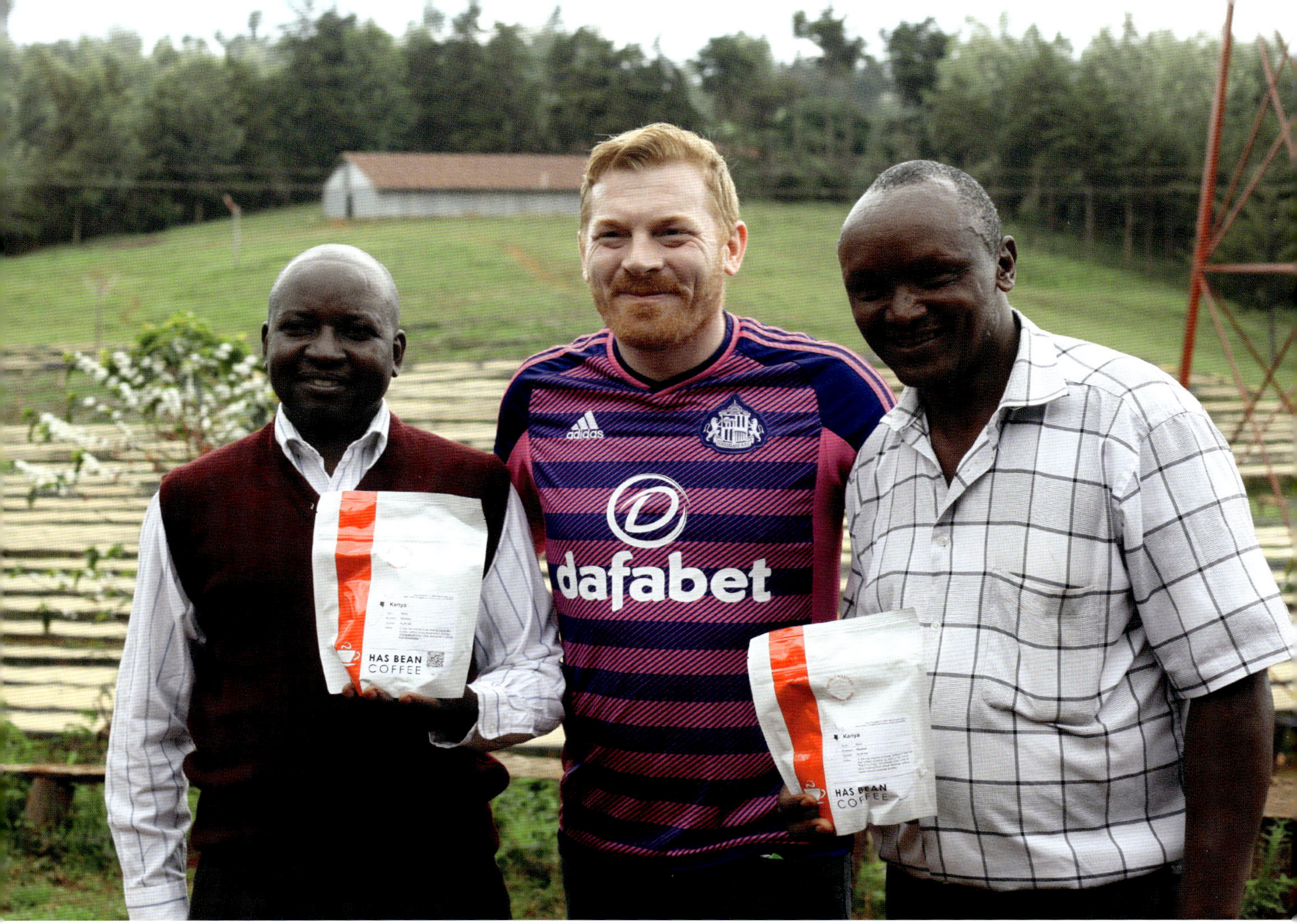

Charles Gathaiya Murimi

So this one is a little bit different to all the other entries in this book. This is someone who is not primarily a farm owner, but the chairman of a cooperative I've been working with for a few years now. His name is Charles Gathaiya Murimi, and he represents the members who deliver coffee to the Kieni wet mill (factory).

The Kieni mill has some 900 active members. It is a part of the Mugaga Farmers Cooperative Society, and Charles is the mill's chairman. Charles became a coffee farmer as well when he inherited a farm from his parents back in 1995.

In a conversation Charles had with me, he said: "Previously coffee was not well paying, and there was no guarantee of good returns. But currently the coffee industry is paying and one is sure of earning good returns. Also, for the good returns I must produce a large quantity of cherry, but also high quality."

> “Previously coffee was not well paying, and there was no guarantee of good returns. But currently the coffee industry is paying and one is sure of earning good returns. Also, for the good returns I must produce a large quantity of cherry, but also high quality.”

His main aim with the mill is to help his members do exactly this by growing yields, but also maintaining the quality that Kieni has become world-renowned for.

The Kieni wet mill is located in Nyeri in the central highlands of Kenya, at an altitude of 1,700 m.a.s.l.

Nyeri county has cool temperatures and fertile central highlands; it lies between the eastern base of the Aberdare (Nyandarua) mountain range, which forms part of the eastern end of the Great Rift Valley and the western slopes of Mount Kenya. Nyeri town (county headquarters) acts as a destination for those visiting Aberdare National Park and Mount Kenya.

Most of the coffee beans from Nyeri develop and mature slowly because of the unique climate, producing extra hard beans. This quality is also evident in the cup. As a result, Nyeri is traditionally known as the heart of Kenya’s black gold coffee.

Charles works very closely with his mill manager, Josphat Kariuki, who is in charge of the production. The coffee is wet processed. It’s pulped, fermented, washed and then dried slowly over 2–3 weeks.

Both Charles and Josphat are chosen to be in their positions of office by the members: they vote for who should lead the factories and the cooperative as a whole.

On my last visit to Kenya, Charles proudly told me that the members are paid 89 shillings per kg. To put that into some context, the pay at some of the other washing stations we visited was as low as 60 Kenyan shillings per kg of cherry delivered.

These prices have inspired the members to continue to raise their quality in the hope the prices rise. Much of this is due to the professional leadership found at the factory.

NAME: Charles Gathaiya Murimi

AGE: 50

IN COFFEE: 20 yrs

What makes your coffee special: The way it is taken care of by our farmers and their application, and that of our wet mill manager and his team.

Your proudest achievement in coffee: It helps me educate my children and to upkeep my family with ease. Also, when I was elected to represent farmers of Kieni, I managed to stabilise and eradicate the coffee politics of the area.

Tell us something we don't know about you: I am especially interested in what's happening in the world – in particular in the world of politics.

Favourite way to relax: Sipping sweet coffee, silently.

If you could grow coffee anywhere in the world apart from your own country, where and why: Brazil, because the country also lies on the equator, like my farm, so the climate is very similar.

What's your favourite coffee time of the year: Harvesting, because whatever is harvested translates to returns.

If you had a blank cheque, what would be the one investment you would make in the farm: To manure the coffee bushes with enough farmyard manure, to increase the fertiliser application.

Favourite coffee you've had (not including your own): One by our friends from Coffee Collective (Denmark).

Nicaragua

"You never forget your first love, just like you never forget your first coffee origin trip. Nicaragua will always be my special place."

– Stephen Leighton

N I C A R A G U A

It was not until the 1850s that large scale coffee growing began in Nicaragua. But coffee was the principal export crop by 1870: a position it held for the next century. The government of Nicaragua encouraged coffee growing in 1879 by offering 5 cents for each tree in plantations of more than 5,000. Production reached 150,000 bags in 1900, versus 75,000 bags in the preceding year.

Most of this production was managed by a small number of large landowners, and it wasn't until the early 20th century that we began to see growers' cooperatives form and allow smaller landowners to benefit from coffee production.

The 20th century saw civil war, Contra rebel groups targeting the coffee production areas, interference from the USA and the CIA, communism, and general poor living conditions (it has the second poorest economy in the northern hemisphere). But coffee still remains a very important export.

During the coffee price crisis between 1999 and 2003, three of Nicaragua's six banks collapsed due to their exposure to coffee.

Despite this, Nicaraguan coffee has become a more traceable cup and a leader in the speciality world. It has some of the most diverse coffee profiles and producers.

Coffee Facts

Total production in 2016 (60 kg): 2,100,000
Percentage rise and fall on previous year: -1.7%
Internal consumption in 2016 (60 kg): 209,000
Consumption per capita: 2.08 kg per person per annum
Taste profile: Complex, fruity, medium-to-high acidity and sweetness
Common varietals: Typica, Bourbon, Caturra and Pacamara
Coffee growing altitudes: 1,000 m.a.s.l. to 1,700 m.a.s.l.
Rank of coffee production: 12th in the world
Main buyers: Germany, USA and the Netherlands
Unique problems: Drought, leaf rust and climate change
Soil types: Volcanic

Country Facts

Population:
6,217,796 (2017)

Population density:
52 people per km^2

Capital city:
Managua

Land mass:
120, 353 km^2

Currency:
Córdoba

NICARAGUA

Finca Las Delicias

"Our dedication to the small details is what makes us different. We know that quality is not synonymous with quantity. We focus on producing the best quality possible while utilising the best practices."

"I feel so proud when we are cupping with our clients and we see the satisfaction on their faces."

Eleane Mierisch

Eleane is so unique. Without years of being involved in speciality coffee, she has become one of the leading lights in coffee processing – and now coffee cupping – in what seems like a very short time. Taking advantage of the skills she already had in her "previous life," she has managed to lead in a role that's normally dominated by men.

Although she grew up in one of the most famous coffee families in the world, Eleane did not start her career in coffee. In the 1980s, the Sandinista government confiscated the family coffee farms, forcing the entire family into exile in the United States of America. Turning this negative into a positive, Eleane decided to study to become a nurse.

The family farms were returned to them in 1991/1992 by the Nicaraguan government, and most of the family returned to oversee their recuperation from abandonment.

“Be grateful to Mother Nature, and considerate to the people that help us perform the best job. Everyone’s life is not only improved economically but we create a new family that works with passion to produce the best coffee in Nicaragua, and share that with the world.”

But Eleane was settled in the USA. She began her career and followed her father’s footsteps; he was a gynaecologist. She worked as a women’s healthcare nurse practitioner in the USA for some sixteen years.

Illness of her mother, Maria Ligia McEwan, brought Eleane to a crossroads in life. She returned to Nicaragua to help look after her mother and be closer to her family.

Her brother, Erwin, propelled her to get involved in the family coffee business. From the moment she began tasting the flavours found in a cup of coffee, she was inspired. She wanted to know more about the farms' agricultural management, so she learnt each step of the value/production chain. She applied the skills she had learnt as a nurse and the attention to small details she had used her whole life to working as a team, and to using a multidisciplinary approach to coffee processing at the family mill, Don Estaban.

Mining Erwin’s growing knowledge, they became tutor and student. Eleane learnt everything from picking cherries to the exportation of raw green coffee. It wasn’t long, with her amazing attention to detail and focus on the processing, until Eleane (in Erwin’s own words) “put me to shame.”

She gained valuable experience that she now shares with specialty coffee professionals around the world by consulting and being involved in the Cup of Excellence.

In Eleane’s own words: “Be grateful to Mother Nature, and considerate to the people that help us perform the best job. Everyone’s life is not only improved economically but we create a new family that works with passion to produce the best coffee in Nicaragua, and share that with the world.”

Eleane is an inspirational woman in what is a male dominated world.

NAME: Eleane Mierisch

AGE: 47

IN COFFEE: 10 yrs

Favourite coffee varietal and why: Yellow Pacamara, due to its flavour profile of passion fruit, elegant body, and different layers. It's a coffee with a lot of character.

Biggest challenge facing you today: Low yield on the varieties that our clients demand the most. Additional challenges include fighting against leaf rust, and the climate (related to drying the coffee).

Favourite way to relax: Sitting in my small cabin at Las Delicias and drinking a delicious cup of coffee from my farm.

If you could grow coffee anywhere in the world apart from your own country, where and why: In Mexico, because they have regions that have not been developed yet and produce high quality coffee.

Favourite coffee you've had (not including yours): It is a Java from Peru that actually originated on our farms.

What makes your coffee special: The diversity in exotic varieties; the care and management of each lot; the drying process, which is done with dedication; but the most important thing that makes our coffee special is the love and passion from each and every person involved.

If you had a blank cheque, what would be the one investment you would make in the farm: Bettering the quality of life of the people who live and work on the farms.

NICARAGUA

Finca Limoncillo

"Today, coffee is my passion. My greatest source of entertainment."

Erwin Mierisch

I've now met Erwin Mierisch (senior) a number of times in my visits to Nicaragua, and I only found out through writing this book that his name is Erwin. You see, to me he has always been Dr Mierisch. He is a man to whom you can't help but give respect. It's like going to see the Headmaster at school: you know he's human, but he is also a legend.

Beginning his working life as a medical doctor by profession, Erwin specialised in obstetrics and gynaecology.

He practiced this for 20 years in the United States of America when, in the 1980s, the Sandinista government confiscated the family coffee farms.

When the farms were returned by the Nicaraguan government, he travelled to oversee the recuperation, but still practiced medicine in the USA.

Fifteen years ago he decided to retire to Nicaragua and became involved in the family tradition of coffee production.

"I've learned along the way just how amazing the coffee world is. Today, it's my passion. My greatest source of entertainment. With my medical knowledge in genetics, I've been able to play around with the tissue of coffee!"

I've learnt so many things from writing this book, but Dr Mierisch's son (also called Erwin) recalled this story to me. "Stephen and my family formed an instant friendship from the first time we met. It seemed only fate we should begin working together. Stephen bought Limoncillo's winning Nicaragua Cup of Excellence coffee in 2006 at auction without knowing it originated with our family. I believe that was serendipity at work."

But it's not just Limoncillo that the family own: they own Finca San Jose, Finca Los Milagros, Finca La Escondida, Finca Los Altos, Finca Placeres, Finca El Suspiro and Finca Mama Mina. This large amount of farms means there's a large amount of coffee. Quantity doesn't normally mean quality. But just like his daughter Eleane, Dr Mierisch has taken his vast medical experience and attention to detail, and has transposed it into the world of coffee.

Dr Mierisch's real home is the machine shop. Truly hands on, there are few hurdles that he can't overcome. Constantly tweaking and improving, his favourite place is designing, modifying, and machining equipment. It's probably cheaper to buy something new, but where's the fun in that? As you walk around the farms and mill, there are so many Frankenstein machines he has pieced together.

To get an idea of size, let's focus on Finca Limoncillo. The farm is in Matagalpa and, at 171 hectares, it boasts 9 waterfalls on the farm and is home to 60 families full time. Staff get paid up to 30% above minimum wage, have free housing, and get free electricity from the hydroelectric generator linked to one of the waterfalls. During picking, all workers get free meals (temporary employees too). There are free daycare facilities for families, and there are healthcare facilities, a visiting nurse and a full-time teacher.

So doctor or headmaster, he still scares me, but also inspires me. He's a true leader in the world of specialty coffee.

NAME: Erwin Mierisch

AGE: 72

IN COFFEE: 100 yrs

Your proudest achievement in coffee: Having involved all of my children and grandchildren on this passionate journey of coffee production.

Favourite way to relax: Walking through my farms and seeing the ever-changing environment.

Favourite coffee varietal and why: Java, just because ...

What makes your coffee special and why: The whole family's dedication to each step in the coffee process, and our obsessive attention to detail to obtain quality in the cup.

Biggest challenge facing you today: Maintaining high standards despite the escalating costs of production.

Filter or espresso?: Neither, Americano is my drink of choice.

What's your favourite coffee time of the year: The picking of the red (ripe) cherries. Walking amongst the coffee trees is very special.

If you could grow coffee anywhere in the world apart from your own country, where and why: Japan.

If you had a blank cheque, what would be the one investment you would make in the farm: We can always do more. We have invested in facilities for the people who work with us, but we should always aim for more. I always want a better quality of life for the workers.

Acknowledgements

There are so many thanks to put in here, but the most special thanks must go to all the producers and exporters who contributed here, without whom I would not have been able to write this book. I would also like to give a special mention to all those who are not in these pages. I love you equally as much – maybe I could have you in the next edition?

A special mention to Stephen Hurst and Flori Marin, who taught me all I know about working with coffee producers and how to foster special and long-standing relationships. Without them I know nothing.

To Joanna Alm, who has pushed me all the way to write this book after forming the idea on our Central America trip in 2017. Without her I would have given up months ago. My rock, jag älskar dig.

A special shout out to Team Has Bean, who have heard me wittering on about this for months and still took time to listen. Special mentions to Roland, who always pushes me for more information on our producers (at least now I can say "read the book"); and to Dale and Jenn, who helped so much in the early days of forming my ideas, and with the template for the book.

To Colin Harmon for showing me that any idiot can write a book, and motivating me to get off my behind after publishing his own amazing book. Thank you, brother. If half as many people read this as have read your book, I'm blessed.

Team 3FE, who show trust and support in the coffees we buy together. I hope this is useful, Simon and Monica.

To the international coffee organisation for granting permission to use data figures for each country, and for having an awesome website.

To my editor Rebecca Judd, for correcting my most awful English and grammar and putting up with me bothering her day and night. Without her valuable input, this would be illegible.

To Tentacle Media for the specially commissioned maps and flags, and generally helping me get this to print. They are the unsung heroes of Has Bean who are bombarded with my crazy ideas, only to come back with slightly crazier ones.

And, of course, to you, my customers and people who have bought this book. You allow me to meet these amazing people and do what is the best job in the world. Without you I'd be sat at home being a sad and lonely coffee geek. Instead I'm a sad coffee geek who has people with whom I can share these wild stories. I'm truly blessed with the best home and coffee shop customers in the industry.